Celluloid Adventures 4

Science Fiction Thrills...Horror Chills

Celluloid Adventures 4

Science Fiction Thrills... Horror Chills

Nicholas Anez

Midnight Marquee Press, Inc.
Baltimore, Maryland, USA

Also by Nicholas Anez

Celluloid Adventures 3: Great Movies…Evil Wars
Celluloid Adventures 2: Artistic Triumphs…Box-Office Bombs
Celluloid Adventures: Good Movies...Bad Timing

Fiction (as by Nick Anez)
Pigeon
Ripper's Fog
The Blue Mirror

Thanks to Lee Pfeiffer of Cinema Retro
for many of the photos in this book.

Copyright © 2023 Nicholas Anez
Cover Design: A. Susan Svehla
Interior layout: A. Susan Svehla
Copy Editor: Janet Atkinson

Midnight Marquee Press, Inc., Gary J. Svehla and A. Susan Svehla do not assume any responsibility for the accuracy, completeness, topicality or quality of the information in this book. All views expressed or material contained within are the sole responsibility of the author.

Without limiting the rights under copyright reserved above, no part of this publication may be reproduced, stored in or introduced into a retrieval system, or transmitted, in any form, or by any means (electronic, mechanical, photocopying, recording or otherwise), without the prior written permission of the copyright owner or the publishers of the book.

ISBN 978-1-64430-135-7
Library of Congress Catalog Card Number 2023944138
Manufactured in the United States of America
First Printing August 2023

For Margaret Mary

and

Dr. Sundaresan Sambandam
Dr. Amir Alizadeh

Lon Chaney in the title role of *Son of Dracula*

Table of Contents

8	Foreword
10	Introduction
12	Son of Dracula
29	Alias Nick Beal
40	The Maze
58	Donovan's Brain
68	1984
88	The Mind Benders
98	Crack in the World
108	The Mummy's Shroud
118	The Power
132	Journey to the Far Side of the Sun
146	Brain Drainers: The Groundstar Conspiracy & Who?
171	Capricorn One
186	The Medusa Touch
206	Afterword
208	Appendix

Foreword

For several years now I have been hoping that film historian Nick Anez would do a follow-up volume to his earlier three books published under the umbrella title of *Celluloid Adventures*. This trio of works is devoted to productions he not only so richly embraces and chronicles but which he believes have either been unfairly dished by critics or not fared well at the box-office, these factors often serving to banish them to the cinematic broom closet of the forgotten or the easily dismissed. Nick, however, has an astute and discerning ability—coupled with an engaging and unbridled enthusiasm—to find and champion moments from films that might otherwise be overlooked by both critics and the general public alike and which provide legitimate impetus for their rediscovery and reevaluation.

I first encountered his initial effort, *Celluloid Adventures: Good Movies...Bad Timing*, quite by accident after it was first published in 2006 and quickly not only became hooked on his highly entertaining, as well as his historically reliable, essays on old films, but also sensed that in reading these I had stumbled upon a true kindred spirit whose tastes in yesterday's cinematic treasures so often mirrored my own. In this book Nick succinctly and with great gusto tackles everything from celluloid treatments of Tarzan, James Bond and Wyatt Earp to "A" and "B" Westerns of the 1950s. After having finished this read, there was no doubt in my mind that I had to seek out everything this guy had put down on paper about film and soon had the other two volumes in my hands, *Artistic Triumphs...Box-Office Bombs* and *Great Movies...Evil Wars*.

The newest edition to *Celluloid Adventures* subtitled *Science Fiction Thrills...Horror Chills* and unlike the earlier volumes where he tackled a myriad of film types, he confines his focus here to these genre pictures produced between the years 1943 and 1978, most of which he again believes have been given a short shrift by both the public and media critics alike. Although championing these overlooked productions he does not, however, turn a blind eye to those telltale faults found in some of these movies but nonetheless manages to isolate and champion those elements within the framework and body of these efforts which makes them more than worthy of rediscovery.

The 13 films under discussion are truly an eclectic mix, from *Son of Dracula*, one of Universal Studio's productions of the 1940s and regularly savaged by horror fans incensed by the selection of Lon Chaney, Jr. as the thirsty Count, to such later celluloid explorations of various science-fiction themes including *Donovan's Brain*, *The Mind Benders*, *Crack in the World* and *The Power* in addition to various horror productions such as *The Maze* and *The Mummy's Shroud*. Nick provides a full and fascinating analysis of each of these films with a keen eye to those positive elements heretofore usually ignored. A dedicated researcher with a finely tuned eye to what makes the cinematic experience work, Nick approaches all these productions succinctly with impressive depth and admirable fairness. In addition to discussing original source material for the movies and comparing these to the finished celluloid products, he provides salient notes, performance evaluations and with great insight and analytical savvy dissects what does and does not work and why they deserve re-examination.

I know that I came away from reading this book with a definite plan to both view the films I had never actually seen as well as revisiting those I had been exposed to many years before. By his shrewd and well-supported targeting of the worthiness of these too often forgotten motion pictures he had succeeded in firing up my interest in them.

I hope others feel the same way.

Thanks to Nick, they certainly should.

—Bruce Dettman

Introduction

A professor of literature once defined science fiction as speculative fiction with a scientific basis that inspires the imagination of readers; horror fiction, in contrast, doesn't require a scientific basis and inspires fear within readers. Of course, the two genres often combine to stimulate people's minds along with their fears. This certainly applies not only to literature but to science fiction and horror movies.

In this fourth volume of *Celluloid Adventures*, I concentrate totally on science fiction and horror movies instead of a variety of genres which I did in the first three volumes. These movies, with one exception, were box-office failures. I have a distinct memory of *Crack in the World* opening in a neighborhood theater as a co-feature to an Italian sword-and-sandal movie. I clearly remember seeing *The Power* in a theater that attracted at most a couple of dozen patrons upon its opening night. There were even less people in a theater in which I saw *The Groundstar Conspiracy*. *The Medusa Touch* lasted less than a week at a local theater. I could cite similar experiences for the other movies discussed herein but the point is that these movies failed to find an audience despite their merits. The one exception to this box-office curse is *Capricorn One*, which I include because its success was unexpected.

These movies cover a span of 35 years, from 1943 to 1978, and represent the wide range of themes and ideas that science fiction and horror movies may encompass. As in the previous volumes, I again attempt to provide an informative analysis of each movie along with production details, including information on the personnel in front of and behind the camera. If the movies are based upon novels, the differences between novel and film can be very interesting. Samples of reviews from critics, either contemporaneous or in reference

books, give an indication of the movie's reception upon its release as well as its current reputation. The trade paper, *Variety*, and the *Ultimate Movie Rankings* (*UMR*) website provided information on the respective domestic box-office performance of the movies.

My purpose in writing this book is to hopefully create interest in the movies and perhaps motivate people to search for them. Fortunately, due to home video, most of these movies are still available to be seen. Whether they stimulate viewers' minds and/or their fears depends upon the viewer.

Son of Dracula

Son of Dracula, released in 1943, is the third of Universal's Dracula series, following *Dracula* (1931) and *Dracula's Daughter* (1935). It is also the last of the Universal Dracula films to have an adult storyline. The films featuring Dracula that followed—*House of Frankenstein* (1944) and *House of Dracula* (1945)—were aimed toward a decidedly younger audience. The title of *Abbott and Costello Meet Frankenstein* (1948) speaks for itself. In contrast, *Son of Dracula* is actually distinctive in Universal's horror series of the 1930s and 1940s because it is a love story that, except for its special effects, may have bored youthful fans of horror movies. Another attribute of the movie that makes it different is that it has many qualities of a film noir. Furthermore, it is unique in its atypical depiction of the vampire who has inherited his ancestor's title of Count Dracula. In other Dracula films, the Count is the incarnation of evil under whose power mere mortals are helpless. This Count Dracula is equally evil but is also a pawn in the hands of a sinister woman who intends to manipulate him to achieve her own objective.

The setting of *Son of Dracula* is a Southern town in the United States in the mid-20th century. It is a complex story which perhaps can benefit from descriptions of the main characters and their actions throughout the course

Alucard/Dracula (Lon Chaney) attacks Professor Laslo (J. Edward Bromberg) for a publicity photo.

Frank Stanley (Robert Paige) collapses in the swamp and is saved from the vampire bat by the cross on the gravesite.

of the film. Foremost is Count Alucard, a Hungarian nobleman who arrives at the invitation of Katherine "Kay" Caldwell, whom he met in Budapest. It becomes quickly evident that he is also a vampire who has the ability to change into a bat or a misty vapor. Alucard explains that his home country is barren, but America is filled with potential victims to satisfy his bloodlust. His strategy is to assume ownership of Kay's family plantation, Dark Oaks, from which he intends to establish a colony of vampires with Kay's complicity. He wastes no time and makes Kay's father, Colonel Caldwell, his first victim. Fortunately for the Colonel, he dies of a heart attack and not from the vampire's fangs which would have made him one of the undead. Nevertheless, the Colonel's death clears the way for Alucard's marriage to Kay who inherits the mansion. Immediately assuming control of Dark Oaks, Alucard doesn't conceal his scornful view of mortals and perceives them as helpless with no ability to stop him from realizing his scheme. His egotism and sense of superiority prevent him from recognizing that any living human may be more cunning than he is. He vastly underestimates Kay.

Kay Caldwell is an heiress from an aristocratic family who has the respect of people in her community. But she has a fear of death and a morbid interest in the supernatural. She is aware that Alucard's real name is Dracula and that

Kay Caldwell (Louise Allbritton) doesn't prevent the vampire bat from attacking Queen Zimba (Adeline DeWalt Reynolds).

he is a vampire. It becomes obvious that, prior to his arrival, she had already formed an alliance with Dracula and is now desirous of becoming a vampire. When Frank Stanley's bullets pass through Dracula and kill her, Dracula is able to revive her as a vampire because of her macabre predisposition. As a member of the undead, she has now achieved the immortality that she has always desired and intends to rule over the countryside as a vampire queen. But she doesn't intend for Dracula to be her king. She loves only Frank Stanley and plans to convince Frank to sacrifice his life and his soul because of his love for her. Indeed, she intends to give him no choice but to become her king in the land of the undead.

Frank Stanley is Kay's fiancé and has unsuccessfully attempted to persuade Kay to end her obsession with the occult. After Count Alucard arrives, Frank becomes increasingly angered over the mysterious guest's influence over Kay. When Kay tells him that she has married Alucard, he becomes infuriated, attacks the groom and tries to kill him. However, due to the vampire's apparent invincibility, he kills Kay instead. Frank becomes deranged at the knowledge that he has killed the woman that he has loved since childhood. On the verge of an emotional collapse, he confesses his crime to Dr. Brewster who, after visiting Dark Oaks and talking to Kay, is certain that Frank is suffering from a delusion. But Sheriff Dawes later discovers Kay's dead body and arrests Frank. In his jail cell, Kay surprisingly materializes to Frank, apparently alive but strangely devoid of warmth. He becomes even more incredulous when Kay tells him that while he is still a mortal he must destroy Dracula.

Claire Caldwell is Kay's sister who, unlike Kay, displays grief at her father's sudden death. Claire's inherent goodness serves to balance Kay's malevolence. She is suspicious of Alucard, especially after she and Dr. Brewster search his belongings in the guest house and discover that his suitcases are empty. She misinterprets her sister's apparent closeness to Alucard and believes that Kay will never marry Frank. She refuses to be complicit in the doctor's attempt to declare Kay insane, unaware that he is trying to prevent an unspeakable evil that he feels is impending. Claire's loyalty to Kay is not reciprocated. Indeed, after Kay is apparently killed and Claire states that she intends to cremate her sister's body, her life is in jeopardy from the sister that she loves.

Dr. Harry Brewster is concerned over Kay's inexplicable behavior. He is also suspicious of Alucard's apparent control over Kay, but Judge Simmons rejects his attempt to declare Kay to be insane. When he notices that Alucard spelled backwards is Dracula, he contacts Professor Lazlo, an authority on the occult. Lazlo joins Brewster and convinces the skeptical doctor that vampires truly exist. He also deduces that Alucard is a descendant of the original Count Dracula who was destroyed in the previous century. When a woman brings her child in for treatment for bite marks on his neck, the doctor and professor realize that the vampire has begun his savagery. Together they devise a plan to destroy Dracula, but they underestimate the vampire's craftiness. Only a crucifix saves the two men from horrific deaths. But this is only the beginning of the battle between the vampire and the vampire-hunters.

Sheriff Dawes (Patrick Moriarty) finds Kay's body and arrests Frank (Robert Paige) as Dr. Brewster (Frank Craven) and Judge Simmons (Samuel S. Hinds) look on in astonishment.

The movie's title of *Son of Dracula* suggests that Dracula is the dominant character of the movie, and it is true that his appearance at Dark Oaks sets the stage for all that follows. But Kay and Frank are really the main characters, and it is their relationship that

Frank (Robert Paige) begs for help from Dr. Brewster (Frank Craven) after trying to kill Dracula but shoots Kay instead.

assumes prominence as the film progresses, relegating Dracula to a peripheral though still ominous figure. The main storyline involves Frank's internal struggle to choose between immortality with the woman he loves and losing her forever. Immortality can be very tempting, especially since Kay is the absolute love of his life.

Kay's diabolical plan unfolds as the story evolves. Dracula may be threatening to Brewster and Lazlo but is a pawn in Kay's hands. She achieves the first stage of her plan by becoming a vampire. She does not intend to let anyone prevent her from accomplishing her objective of reigning as queen of the vampires with Frank as her king. According to her plan, they will then be able to prey upon the people in their community who have always admired her family. This may be the only Dracula film in which another character is more evil than he is.

The second stage of Kay's strategy requires Frank to destroy Dracula. In the form of a bat, Kay extracts blood from Frank while he sleeps in his jail cell. When he awakens, she tells him that she has already begun his transformation into a member of the undead. Frank is so overjoyed to see her that he is tempted to accede to her infernal wishes. Certain of his collaboration, she gives him the secret location of Dracula's grave and the knowledge of how to destroy him. When Matt the jailer tells Brewster and Lazlo that he has overheard Frank talking with a woman's voice as well as his own, they realize that Kay has already become a vampire. Sheriff Dawes doesn't believe their story and when Frank escapes, it appears to confirm his guilt. Dawes together with Brewster and Lazlo launch a pursuit of a man whose actions indicate that he is not only guilty of murder but has become totally deranged.

Frank finds Dracula's coffin and sets it afire. A vicious fight with Dracula ensues but the fire combined with the sunrise condemn the vampire king to destruction. Frank has done Kay's bidding which indicates that he may be prepared to become her undead accomplice. He knows where to find her body which is in her playroom at the mansion, a room filled with her childhood toys, the room in which she was once an innocent child. He gazes lovingly upon her quiescent body in her coffin and gently places his ring upon her finger, sym-

Frank (Robert Paige) pleads with Claire (Evelyn Ankers) not to have Kay cremated while Deputy Mac (Walter Sande) tries to calm him down.

Kay (Louise Allbritton) enters Queen Zimba's shack in the heart of the swamp.

bolizing their marriage. But this act is a prelude to his final act of love. When Brewster, Lazlo and Dawes arrive, they see that he has set fire to her coffin, thus freeing her soul from Dracula's evil as well as her own evil. As her body turns to ashes, Frank can only stare dejectedly. He has saved Kay's soul but has destroyed the only woman that he will ever love. His expression reflects complete misery, and it is doubtful that he will ever fully recover from the horrific events that have occurred.

Robert Siodmak directed *Son of Dracula* from a screenplay by Eric Taylor which is based upon an original story by Curtis Siodmak, the director's broth-

Belgian poster for *Son of Dracula*

er. In Curt's autobiography, *Wolf Man's Maker: Memoir of a Hollywood Writer* (Scarecrow Press; 2001), he writes: "When Robert was offered the direction, he was in financial despair (and) was offered a weekly salary of only $150." Because Curt had written the original story, he expected to write the screenplay. However, when Robert signed on to direct the movie, he asked producer Ford

Beebe to fire his brother and hire another writer. Curt writes: "I was shocked at having lost my job but I understood that he was aware that we could not work together. Who was going to prevail?"

Based upon the résumés of the two writers, the excellence of the script may be due more to Curt Siodmak. Among Curt's previous original screenplays were *The Wolf Man* (1941), the title character quickly becoming one of Universal's iconic monsters. Incidentally, for that movie, Curt created the famous stanza: "Even a man who is pure at heart, And says his prayers by night, May become a wolf when the wolfbane blooms, And the autumn moon is bright." Curt also co-wrote with Ardel Wray the screenplay for *I Walked with a Zombie* (1943) for producer Val Lewton. Though Eric Taylor wrote the original story basis for *The Ghost of Frankenstein* (1942), an underrated entry in the Frankenstein series, he was known primarily for writing or co-writing scripts for B movies and for various crime series (*Ellery Queen*, *Dick Tracy*, *Crime Doctor*, etc.) However, since he has sole screenplay credit for *Son of Dracula*, he should probably share the acclaim for its distinction. (The chapter on *Donovan's Brain* contains additional information on Curt Siodmak.)

Regardless of the respective contributions of the two writers to the final screenplay, *Son of Dracula* features a Dracula that has an uncharacteristic human failing. Other portrayals of the character personify extreme evil and are only susceptible to the usual artifacts of the legend, such as sunlight and a wooden stake. But though sunlight destroys the vampire of *Son of Dracula*, the primary instrument of his destruction is essentially his failing to detect that Kay might be more devious than he is. Thus, this inhuman monster is destroyed by his own human vanity. The film's two other major characters are equally atypical. Kay Caldwell, unlike the usual female lead in a Dracula movie, dominates all of the other characters with her deceit. Her obsession with the supernatural creates a frightening and depraved character who will kill anybody, including those who love her, to achieve her objective. Frank Stanley, unlike the standard protagonist, displays a vulnerability that makes him equally uncharacteristic. The events that transpire push him to the brink of instability. An indication of his weakness is that he vacillates when Kay tempts him with her plan for immortality, thus revealing that his love for her has morally crippled him.

Robert Siodmak's direction breathes atmosphere. Assisted by George Robinson's murky photography, many scenes suggest a steadily increasing mood of despair and doom. This mood is initially exemplified by the external shot of Dark Oaks which in the nighttime appears besieged by the threatening woodlands surrounding it. The intimation of impending doom, despite the apparent gaiety of the party inside, anticipates the arrival of Alucard who will in a later scene be introduced outside of the mansion. An equally atmospheric sequence occurs when Kay hastens through the woods in search of Queen Zimba, the practitioner of voodoo. The trees and branches of the swampland seem to

Lon Chaney poses menacingly as Count Alucard/Dracula for a publicity photo.

foreshadow danger. Zimba's warning of impending menace has no effect on Kay, nor does the appearance of the bat that causes Zimba's death. This is the first indication of Kay's decadence. One of the film's most haunting scenes occurs when Dracula's coffin arises from the swamp and the vampire king then materializes from the mist to glide across the quagmire atop his coffin to greet a rapturous Kay. Her obvious excitement and anticipation of immortality in this scene is a perverted component of her fatal obsession.

It is not surprising that Siodmak would become one of the prime exponents of film noir. The style that he would assume in future noir films, such as *The Strange Affair of Uncle Harry* (1945) and *The Killers* (1946), for which he would receive an Academy Award nomination as Best Director, is on display here. Once Kay assumes ownership of the stately mansion, the interiors that shone so brightly when the Colonel was alive now seem oppressive due to the shadowy photography and expressionistic lighting that complements the new proprietress and her groom. Many scenes take place at night and add to the sense of desolation that permeates the film. The characters are equally reminiscent of noir movies. Dracula is the supreme villain and predator who reigns not in the criminal underworld but in the world of the undead. Kay is the ultimate noir femme fatale who manipulates not only Frank but Dracula. Kay's fear of death evokes the portent of fatality that is so familiar in film noir. Her discontent with her mortal life along with her sense of superiority is reflected by her disdainful attitude toward anyone that doesn't share her supernatural beliefs. Frank Stanley is an archetypal noir victim whom Kay extracts from his secure world and plunges into a world of confusion and anguish. Dracula's inflexible evil, Kay's adamant cynicism and Frank's doomed romanticism combined with the stylish direction and stark imagery create a perfect example of horror-noir.

John P. Fulton's special effects were quite innovative in 1943. This was the first movie to show a vampire changing into a bat and vice-versa. The effects were realistic for the time and are still admirable today. Incidentally, that same year Fulton received his third nomination for an Academy Award for his special effects for Universal's *Invisible Agent*. He would eventually win two Oscars for *Wonder Man* (1945) and *The Ten Commandments* (1956). The score by Hans J. Salter, Universal's music director and the recipient of four Academy Award nominations, also deserves mention. He noticeably utilizes the studio's stock music to underscore many scenes, but it is effective. Salter's main theme heard under the titles is suitably eerie and perfectly complements the gruesome acts depicted throughout the movie. The romantic theme is particularly memorable, especially in the concluding sequence. The music is initially soft and gentle as Frank gazes upon the sleeping Kay and then gradually soars until the camera closes in on his totally desolate appearance, thus adding tremendously to the emotionalism of the finale. Universal's entire production crew, including the set decorator and art decorator, also deserve credit for the movie's sustained mood of despondency as well as its accurate settings. It is difficult to believe that the realistic swamplands and woodlands as well as Dark Oaks are all on the studio's backlot. And Saul Goodkind's editing keeps the movie down to a crisp 80 minutes with not a single pointless moment.

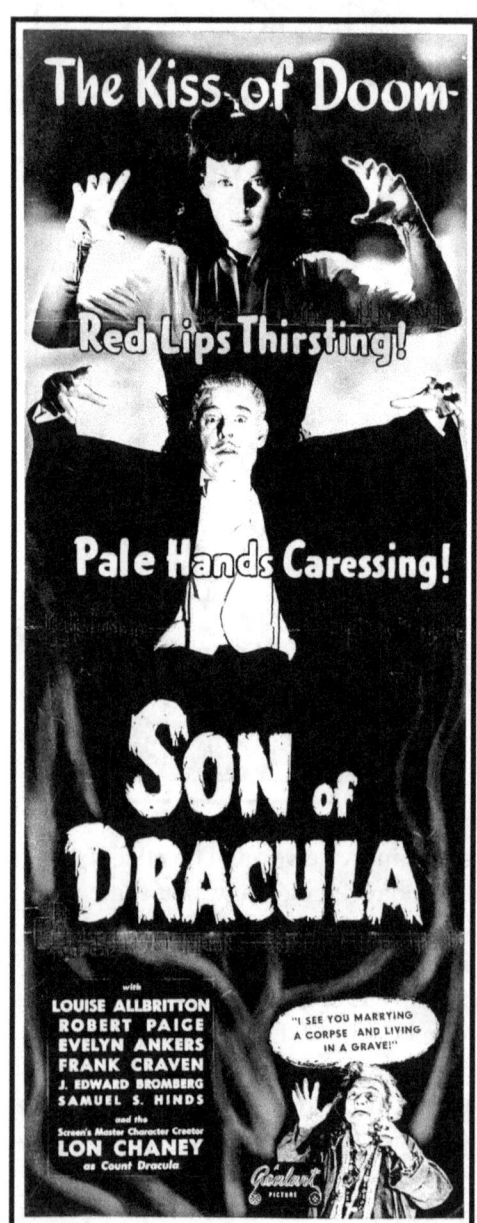

Lon Chaney (he had dropped the "Jr." two years earlier) has received some criticism for his portrayal of Dracula due to his robust stature and midwestern accent but it is undeserved. It is true that in his novel, Bram Stoker describes Dracula as "tall and slender", but Chaney is playing Dracula's descendant. He puts his own stamp on the role and creates a formidable character with a bestial rage and a menacing gaze that can instill fear in any mortal. As his character assumes control over Dark Oaks, Chaney provides him with contemptuous arrogance in his dealings with mortals. The actor is especially effective in the film's penultimate sequence in which Dracula displays both fury and fear as he faces his destruction from fire and sunlight. Chaney's interpretation of Dracula is distinctive and notable.

In his autobiography, Curt Siodmak writes: "Lon Chaney was wrongly cast; Bela Lugosi should have played the part." This suggests that Curt probably intended for the vampire to be the original Count himself. However, if Lugosi had starred, the movie would have been entirely different and not as distinctive. Lugosi was 61 years old at the time and looked older. Louise Allbritton, who played Kay, was only 23 years

old so the pairing would have been implausible. Chaney was 36 years old and a far better match as Allbritton's mate. Curt writes further about Chaney's misbehavior due to excessive alcohol intake and this may have influenced Curt's opinion. Regardless, Chaney's performance should be judged independently of his personal problems.

Though Chaney receives special billing in the credits, Robert Paige as Frank Stanley is the center of the film, and he is superb. It is a difficult character to credibly portray because Frank is a man who must undergo several variations as he is forced to confront the incredible reality that the woman he loves has become a vampire. Paige credibly changes from standard leading man to rejected suitor to inadvertent killer to unstable victim and finally to a heroic but empty shell of a man. It is an inspired performance that is genuinely award-worthy, but such recognition was impossible for a horror movie, especially one that was probably considered a routine B movie. Louise Allbritton as Kay Caldwell complements Paige quite believably. With her silky voice and subdued manner, she cleverly conveys Kay's duplicity which makes her treacherous scheme quite likely to succeed. Though the actress is handicapped by having to project a consistent iciness for her character, she nevertheless manages to make Kay not only odious and despicable but eventually pathetic in view of the surroundings she chooses for her repose. Incidentally, in advertisements for the movie, Allbritton's name precedes Paige's name but in the film itself Paige's name is first.

Dr. Brewster attempts to persuade Claire to co-sign an insanity complaint against Kay.

Evelyn Ankers has little to do as Claire, but she manages to make her character sympathetic and an effective counterpart to Kay. Frank Craven as Dr. Brewster and J. Edward Bromberg as Professor Lazlo are very convincing as intrepid adversaries for Dracula. Samuel S. Hinds as Judge Simmons, Adeline DeWalt Reynolds as Queen Zimba, Pat Moriarty as Sheriff Dawes and Walter Sande as Mac all help to make the horrific proceedings believable with their brief but convincing performances. There are thankfully no comedy interludes in the movie to offset the steadily growing feeling of dread that permeates the story from beginning to end.

Reference books generally—but not always—praise *Son of Dracula*. In *Horror Movies: An Illustrated Survey* (Secker & Warburg; 1967), Carlos Clarens writes that it is "directed to great effect by Robert Siodmak." William K. Everson in *Classics of the Horror Film* (Citadel Press; 1974) calls it "a restrained and intelligent thriller, somewhat shy of the sustained horror set pieces that the aficionados expected but with good dialogue, plot construction and one or two exceptionally devised pictorial special effects to compensate." In *The Encyclopedia of Horror Movies* (Harper & Row; 1986), Phil Hardy praises the sequence of the coffin emerging from the lake but criticizes "a script stronger on character, dialogue and situation than on incident." Hardy or whoever wrote this critique (the book has additional contributors) adds: "Neither Chaney nor Allbritton bring much subtlety or passion to the morbidly erotic side of their relationship in which she ecstatically embraces vampirism in order to share immortality with him." This last sentence indicates that the writer's memory is faulty because Allbritton

Lon Chaney and Louise Allbritton pose for a publicity photo.

is not supposed to display passion for Chaney whom she plans to destroy; thus, the criticism is unjustified.

Son of Dracula did not make much of an impact at the box-office. At the end of the year, *Variety* listed each studio's financial successes along with the individual movie's domestic theatrical rentals, which were approximately one-half of the gross. Universal lists 13 movies in the hit category including *The Phantom of the Opera* ($1.6 million), which is as much a musical as a horror movie, and *Flesh and Fantasy* ($1.8 million), which is an anthology movie containing three supernatural stories. The studio's list does not include *Son of Dracula* or *Frankenstein Meets the Wolf Man* which was also released that year. It is probable that moviegoers who were enduring the real horrors of World

War II were not interested in fictional monsters. The only true horror movie to make the grade from all of the studios is RKO's *Cat People* ($1.2 million). It is informative that the biggest hits of the year were the Spanish Civil War drama, *For Whom the Bell Tolls* ($11 million), the religious drama, *The Song of Bernadette* ($7 million) and the musical comedy salute to the troops, *This Is the Army* ($7 million). In stark contrast, the *UMR* website provides the total gross of *Son of Dracula* as a mere $263,353.

Nevertheless, *Son of Dracula* is a vastly underrated horror movie that is also a romantic tragedy. It is a true gem in the horror film genre.

Credits: Producer: Ford Beebe; Director: Robert Siodmak; Screenplay: Eric Taylor, based upon a story by Curt Siodmak; Cinematographer: George Robinson; Editor: Saul A. Goodkind; Music: Hans J. Salter; Special Effects: John P. Fulton; Art Direction: John B. Goodman, Martin Obzina; Set Decoration: Martin A. Gausman, Edward R. Robinson; Costumes: Vera West

Cast: Lon Chaney (Alucard/Dracula); Robert Paige (Frank Stanley); Louise Allbritton (Katherine "Kay" Caldwell); Evelyn Ankers (Claire Caldwell); Frank Craven (Doctor Harry Brewster); J. Edward Bromberg (Professor Lazlo); Samuel S. Hinds (Judge Simmons); Adeline DeWalt Reynolds (Madame Zimba); Pat Moriarty (Sheriff Dawes); George Irving (Colonel Caldwell); Etta MacDaniel (Sarah); Cyril Delavanti (Coroner); Robert Dudley (Justice of the Peace)

Alias Nick Beal

District Attorney Joseph Foster is so frustrated over his inability to convict local racketeer Hansen that he angrily states that he would give his soul to put the gangster behind bars. He will learn to regret those words because someone will take him up on his offer. That someone is quite literally diabolical. And Foster will learn that the price of his soul will be eternal suffering.

Paramount released the movie, *Alias Nick Beal*, in 1949. It stars Ray Milland, Audrey Totter and Thomas Mitchell. John Farrow directed the screenplay by Jonathan Latimer based upon a story by Mindret Lord. It is the story of a good man with noble intentions but whose ambitions make him susceptible to corruption. A familiar story perhaps but the purveyor of the corruption in this tale epitomizes evil. A clue to his identity occurs during the opening credits of the movie which take place amidst a nighttime rainstorm accompanied by lightning and thunder. As the title suggests, Nick Beal is just an alias. His real name is Lucifer, also known as Satan.

Can such a demonic being actually exist? When Foster's close friend Reverend Garfield mentions such a possibility, Foster laughs off the suggestion. After all, he says, this is the 20th century; no one actually believes anymore in such a creature complete with horns and a tail. But why does Foster look so dejected during the first scene of the movie as he ascends the steps to be sworn in as Governor? This is the fulfillment of his dream. He should

be ecstatic. For the answer to that question, the film flashes back eight months to the beginning of his nightmare.

Joseph Foster is a district attorney with an impeccable reputation for honesty. When local mobster Frankie Faulkner tries to bribe him, Foster throws him out of his office. This type of noble act endears him to his devoted wife, Martha, and to his three staunch supporters: Reverend Garfield, Judge Hobson and Paul Norton. Foster is also a sponsor of a club for wayward boys that Reverend Garfield manages. He unselfishly takes the time out of his busy schedule to try to help delinquent Larry Price. Though the Reverend sympathizes with Foster's disappointment over his failed case against Hansen, he initially dismisses his friend's rash offer to sacrifice his soul for justice as a thoughtless remark. Of course, Foster was only speaking figuratively but almost immediately after his reckless statement, he receives an invitation to meet someone at a waterfront dive called the China Coast Café. This anonymous caller promises to give him incriminating evidence against Hansen. Both the Reverend and Martha caution him against meeting this caller, but he rejects their advice.

That evening, a man appears mysteriously out of the fog-enshrouded dock on the waterfront. Dressed elegantly in a black suit, he looks like a debonair gentleman, the kind of man who doesn't belong in a dingy bar. But he enters the China Coast Café and snobbishly displays disdain toward the bartender as he orders a rare liquor. When Foster comes in shortly thereafter and joins him, the man gives the district attorney a card with the words: "Nicholas Beal,

Agent." He offers to give Hansen's financial books to Foster, though Foster had heard that the racketeer's bookkeeper, a man named Lynch, had destroyed the books. Furthermore, Beal appears to have obtained the books illegally. Foster is so anxious to imprison Hansen that, despite his misgivings, he takes the books. His ambition and pride have assumed precedence over his conscience. This will be the first step of his corruption by Mr. Beal.

Following his successful prosecution of Hansen, Foster's friends eagerly encourage him to run for governor. Needing time to ponder, he retreats to his library and is surprised to find Nick Beal waiting for him. Beal has the uncanny knack of appearing mysteriously, as if out of nowhere and then disappearing just as suddenly. Foster disregards his wife's advice to stay away from Beal, whom she dislikes and distrusts. He also ignores Reverend Garfield who senses something strange about Beal and feels that he has met him before. Nevertheless, Foster accepts Beal's tempting donation to his campaign, falling deeper into Beal's trap. Interestingly, at a meeting at the boys' club, when the Reverend reads a passage from the Bible, he detects a clue to Beal's identity when Beal displays a combination of fear and anger before hastily leaving the room.

Beal increasingly intrudes upon Foster's life, tempting him with political success, power and sex. His intricate plan requires a woman, and he recruits Donna Allen, a former aspiring actress whose prior involvement in a scan-

Nick Beal (Ray Miland) will not let Donna Allen (Audrey Totter) forget what she owes for her new life of luxury.

British poster for *Alias Nick Beal*

dal has plunged her into alcoholism and prostitution. She is so destitute that she cannot resist Beal's offer of a luxurious apartment complete with a new wardrobe. Under Beal's guidance, she poses as a wealthy donor and eventually becomes Foster's campaign manager. Foster now craves the governorship, ostensibly to have the authority to do good deeds. Aware of Foster's ambition, Beal persuades him to form an alliance with Frankie Faulkner. This causes his friends to lose faith in him and disavow their support. Foster also succumbs physically to Donna's allure. Beal then coerces Faulkner's former bookkeeper, Lynch, to come out of hiding and do his bidding. Beal kills Lynch, frames Foster for the crime and then promises to prevent his arrest in return for his signature on a vaguely confusing contract. Beal's strategy succeeds and Foster is elected governor, but he has lost his wife, his friends and his integrity. All he has left to lose is his soul which he has placed in jeopardy due to the ambiguous contract that Beal persuaded him to sign.

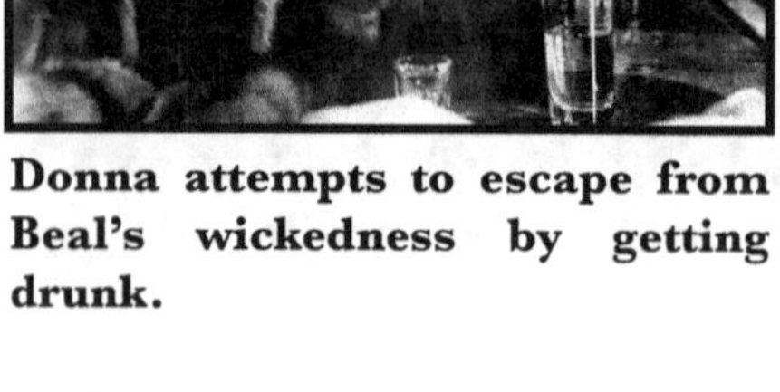

Donna attempts to escape from Beal's wickedness by getting drunk.

Alias Nick Beal is a supernatural horror story, but director John Farrow avoids the usual trappings of the genre. There are no overtly frightening scenes in the movie. The monster doesn't have the facial features of a goat but instead is physically attractive. The horror quotient is subliminal but steadily intensifies as the identity of the mysterious Mr. Beal becomes increasingly evident. His ability to maneuver people and to predict the course of events inspires mounting fear within the characters who are directly affected by his manipulations. Due to Farrow's astute direction, viewers have the same fearful reaction because the director downplays the fantastic elements while revealing just enough of Beal's warped machinations to keep audiences hooked without straining credibility. The director maintains this delicate balance between the realistic and the fantastic by initially emphasizing Beal's human qualities while minimizing his paranormal abilities. He does an expert job of building tension and suspense by grounding the events in familiar settings. This creates a truly terrifying experience because the other characters are identifiable and belong in the real world, not a fantastic one.

The movie also fits within the category of a film noir. Farrow had previously directed such noirs as *The Big Clock* (1948) and *Night Has a Thousand Eyes* (1948) which were his first two collaborations with writer Jonathan Latimer. Latimer had also written *The Glass Key* (1942) and *They Won't Believe Me* (1947), among other noirs. Farrow and Latimer made a good team which is evident

Beal invades Joseph Foster's (Thomas Mitchell) life.

Science Fiction Thrills...Horror Chills

from their third film together. Latimer's screenplay for *Alias Nick Beal* depicts an honest man who is attempting to prevent criminal elements from exploiting defenseless members of the community. However, he commits the disastrous mistake of inviting a far more sinister evil into the society that he is trying to protect. As the story progresses, Foster's plight becomes increasingly hopeless in part because his fall from grace is due not only to his evil nemesis but also to his vanity and ambition. His gradual loss of control over his life and his destiny make him a prime noir character. His future is symbolized when he cannot find ice for his drink and Beal sarcastically tells him, "There is no ice, my friend," referring to the destination that he has planned for his victim. That destination has many names, but Beal calls it Armus Pardidas, which Reverend Garfield translates as the Island of Lost Souls. This is the noir world at its darkest.

Farrow's direction is vastly aided by Lionel Lindon's atmospheric photography. Lindon frequently utilizes low camera angles to emphasize Beal's increasingly dominating influence over both Foster and Donna Allen. Many scenes boldly contrast light with darkness to emphasize Beal's dark intrusion into Foster's environment and into his previously uncorrupted character. The fact that key exterior scenes occur at nighttime with even interior scenes being shrouded in a dark aura creates a feeling of impending doom. The use of thick fog, a mainstay of noir, is particularly effective for the waterfront scenes not only to highlight Beal's ominous introduction but his despondent exit at the climax. Also deserving of mention is Franz Waxman's eerie score which perfectly complements the unnatural visuals.

Ray Milland gives an exceptional performance as Nick Beal. At this time, Milland had been one of Paramount's most popular actors for over a decade, proving his versatility in various genres such as comedies (*The Major and the Minor*; 1942), action films (*Reap the Wild Wind*; 1942), dramas (*Till We Meet Again*; 1944) and thrillers (*Ministry of Fear*; 1944). In 1945, he won a Best Actor Academy Award for his portrayal of an alcoholic in *The Lost Weekend* and subsequently became the studio's highest-paid actor. In 1946, he made his first movie with John Farrow, *California*, a Western which was a popular hit. In 1948, he again worked with Farrow on *The Big Clock*, a critical as well as popular success.

Alias Nick Beal was the third of four movies that Milland made with Farrow and, as the title character, he is effectively sinister and devious, callous and malevolent. It is a daring performance because his character has absolutely no redeeming qualities and represents the epitome of evil. Very few leading actors, especially those accustomed to playing heroic and likeable characters, would risk alienating their fans with such a portrayal. Interestingly, it could very well have been a one-dimensional interpretation, but Milland provides his character with distinct nuances during key scenes. Note his distress when he hears the spiritual words from the Bible. Note his threatening expression when he says that he doesn't like being touched. Note his intense fury when he violently strikes Donna upon being propositioned by her. And take special note of his triumphant smile when Foster's conscience resurfaces, thus violating the

Italian poster for *Alias Nick Beal*

contract and sealing his fate. Beal delights in corrupting good people, enjoys their agony and looks forward to condemning them to everlasting sorrow. Milland brilliantly imparts this cold-blooded ruthlessness. And yet in the very last scene and with his final words, the actor displays a possible reason for his cruelty, one that elicits not sympathy but possibly some degree of understanding and perhaps even pity. The actor cleverly reflects all of these possible emotions with his tone and expression. Milland's performance is one of his best in his seven-decade-long career.

Audrey Totter had previously appeared in such film noirs as *Lady in the Lake* (1947) and *The Unsuspected* (1947). As Donna Allen, she provides a compelling portrayal of a woman who has reached the depths of despair. Upon her introduction, Donna has hit rock bottom and Totter's expression conveys total desolation. As she succumbs to Beal's requirements, she initially suggests disbelief over the upturn of her life and then escalating concern over Beal's unusual capabilities. When she begins to suspect something amiss with her enigmatic benefactor, she becomes increasingly apprehensive. One key sequence showcases the actress' skill. When Foster visits her and says the exact lines that Beal had foretold, her sensitive eyes reflect a succession of amazement, shock and terror. Totter is also excellent in the subsequent scene at the barroom in which she drunkenly tries to forget Beal's wickedness along with his brutality and then freezes in fear as he suddenly appears and she realizes that she cannot escape his trap.

Thomas Mitchell is equally fine as Joseph Foster. Mitchell, who had won a Best Supporting Actor Academy Award for *Stagecoach* (1939), was one of Hollywood's most talented character actors. He gave memorable performances in such renowned films as *Gone with the Wind* (1939) and *It's a Wonderful Life* (1946). He capably conveys Foster's integrity as well as his failings. He is particularly effective in expressing his character's remorse in his speech of resignation from the position that he had won dishonestly. However, the actor has one handicap that affects his credibility in the role. Foster is supposed to be 48 years old and Mitchell, who was 57 at the time of filming, looks his age and even older. While he is acceptable as Martha's middle-aged husband, he seems mismatched with

Beal recruits the alcoholic prostitute Donna Allen to pose as a wealthy donor.

Totter, who was 32 years old. A less mature actor perhaps would have also more believably suggested Foster's sexual ardor. This serves not to diminish Mitchell's acting credentials but only to illustrate the importance of casting based on suitability and not popularity.

The supporting actors all contribute to the film's plausibility by the sincerity of their portrayals. George Macready, frequently cast as refined villains in such noirs as *My Name is Julia Ross* (1945) and *Gilda* (1946) as well as *The Big Clock*, is cast against type as Reverend Garfield but yet projects piety quite proficiently. Though Fred Clark would later be noted for comedy roles, he often played villains early in his career and is aptly slimy as Frankie Faulkner. Geraldine Wall's role as the loyal Martha is in part a thankless one but she effectively creates a portrait of emotional strength and support to balance her husband's fallibility.

The review of *Alias Nick Beal* in *The New York Times* was favorable but still critical: "This is an arresting, expertly-tuned morality drama calculated to hold attention (but) reservation is taken on the grounds that the writers and director failed to bring their picture to as successful and convincing a conclusion as one had been led to expect." The review in *Variety* was positive but forecast troubles at the box-office: "Despite the general excellence of the interpretation by all concerned, there is an unreal quality about it that makes popular reception doubtful." The trade paper's prognosis proved to be correct.

Variety's list of top grossers of 1949 includes 92 movies which earned more than the minimum of $1,500,000 in domestic theatrical rentals. Despite Ray Milland's popularity, *Alias Nick Beal* did not earn enough to qualify for a position on the list. It's possible that audiences simply didn't want to see the actor portraying such a demonic character. Or perhaps they didn't want to see Lucifer portrayed in any fashion due to his horrid connotations. By means of comparison, the top grossing movies on the list are *Jolson Sings Again*, *Pinky* and *I Was a Male War Bride* with theatrical rentals between $5.5 million and $4 million. It is informative that an accompanying article states that "subject matter and story predominated over stars in bringing patrons to theaters." Incidentally, *It Happens Every Spring*, a comedy starring Milland, is 58th on the list with $1,800,000.

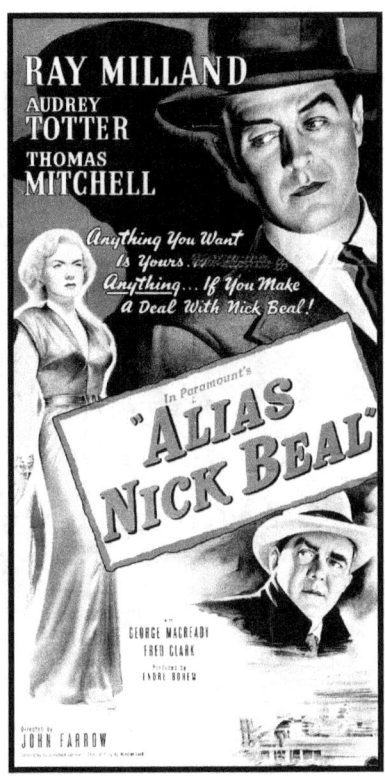

The ending of *Alias Nick Beal* is satisfying in that good defeats evil. The ending also exposes another aspect of Beal's character. Because of the power of the Bible, Beal must withdraw and return to his domain without Foster. He tells Foster that all human beings contain their own seed of destruction, their own weakness. And then he adds: "You know that now, Foster; you're lucky, luckier than I was when I fell—that was a long time ago." With these words, Beal reveals a hint of bitterness and perhaps regret for his downfall as well as his resignation to his fate. He must return to the Island of Lost Souls, where he rules over other souls who are doomed to exist forever in pain and misery.

However, he will be back, looking to condemn others to a similar existence of endless suffering. He may have a different name and a different appearance. But he will be back. Count on it.

Credits: Producer: Endre Bohem; Director: John Farrow; Screenplay: Jonathan Latimer, based upon a story by Mindret Lord; Cinematographer: Lionel Lindon; Editing Supervisor: Eda Warren; Music: Franz Waxman; Art Direction: Franz Bachelin, Hans Dreier; Set Decoration: Sam Comer, Ross Dowd; Costumes: Mary Kay Dodson

Cast: Ray Milland (Nick Beal); Audrey Totter (Donna Allen); Thomas Mitchell (Joseph Foster); George Macready (Reverend Garfield); Geraldine Wall (Martha Foster); Fred Clark (Frankie Faulkner); Douglas Spencer (Finch); Henry O'Neill (Judge Hobson); Darryl Hickman (Larry Price); Nestor Paiva (Bartender); Charles Evans (Paul Norton); Arlene Jenkins (Maid)

The Maze

Allied Artists released *The Maze* in 1953. The movie is a hybrid of sorts. It is a horror movie, a science fiction movie, a suspense movie and a romance. It is also an extremely sorrowful story. Furthermore, the legendary production designer, William Cameron Menzies, directed it in 3-Dimension.

Maurice Sandoz's novel

Any discussion of the movie should start with its origin. The Glamis Castle in Scotland is the setting of a legend which states that, at some time in the distant past, the titled family that lived in the castle gave birth to a gruesomely deformed monster that was hidden away for all of its life. According to the legend, the mystery of the misshapen occupant whose lifespan exceeded that of normal human beings was passed down from generation to generation, members of which became caretakers of the secret lodger. In the 19th century, this mystery was allegedly the subject of furtive conversations throughout Europe's royal families. Variations of the story eventually filtered down to the general population, either as fact or rumor. The narrative usually involved secret chambers, locked doors, ritual initiations and sightings of a malformed creature seen on the castle's parapets at nighttime. Most accounts refer to the creature as being grotesquely inhuman with some being more specific in their description of a monster that was half-man and half-toad.

It was inevitable that such as legend would generate fictional interpretations. Maurice Sandoz (1892-1958) was born in Switzerland and earned a doctorate in chemistry but was also a writer and composer. The legend of the Glamis Monster inspired him to write his most famous novel, *The Maze*, which Doubleday Doran published in 1945. The original edition of the novel included illustrations by surrealist artist Salvadore Dali and in mint condition is now a collector's item. The novel is fairly short—110 pages—and is reminiscent in style of works by H.P. Lovecraft, particularly in its gradual development of mystery and horror. It begins in the present with an unidentified narrator—presumably the author—who recounts his meeting with an elderly woman, Mrs. Edith Murray, while recuperating from an illness in the Swiss Alps. Edith proceeds to tell her story which she admits that the young narrator may find

Science Fiction Thrills...Horror Chills

preposterous. It begins several years earlier but her memory of the startling events is so vivid that she remembers each detail and each line of dialogue.

Edith's cousin, Gerald MacTeam, is engaged to Kitty Murray, her godchild and niece. Following his uncle's death, Gerald returns to his Scottish ancestral home of Craven Castle. After a lengthy period, Edith receives a letter from Gerald asking her to tell Kitty that he cannot marry her. This news shatters Kitty but angers Edith who finds Gerald's cruel behavior uncharacteristic. Upon researching the history of Craven Castle, Edith learns that none of the baronets ever married and that the title was passed down from uncle to nephew for generations. Also, the uncles all died at a relatively young age. Gerald eventually invites Edith to come to the castle for a grouse hunt along with other guests, including Gerald's friend, Harry Seymour. Upon arriving at the castle, Edith is surprised to see that Gerald has seemingly aged while his usually pleasant demeanor has become morose and sullen. She is also puzzled by strange sounds in the middle of the night and mysterious nighttime lights in the intricate maze next to the castle. After a death in the family and a secret burial, Gerald provides a solution to the mystery for Edith which leads to a happy ending for Gerald and Kitty.

Allied Artists, previously Monogram Pictures, owned the film rights to the novel. In 1953, the management of Allied Artists was determined to elevate the status of the former poverty row studio. Under the guidance of executive producer Walter Mirisch, AA began to produce films with higher budgets and talented personnel. Mirisch also decided to jump on the 3-D bandwagon. The previous November, the box-office success of *Bwana Devil*, the first 3-D

Gerald MacTeam (Richard Carlson) drinks to control his anger due to his uninvited guests.

movie and an independent production, stunned the film industry. Despite the requirement of special glasses which major studio chiefs figured would deter audiences, the movie was so successful in its initial engagements that United Artists acquired distribution rights. By the beginning of 1953, all of the studios were preparing 3-D movies. Warner Bros. was rushing production of the horror movie, *House of Wax*, which would be the first major studio movie in 3-D.

In February 1953, Mirisch announced that the film version of *The Maze* would be Allied Artists' first production to utilize the 3-D process. He also announced that the movie would incorporate in some way Salvadore Dali's drawings for the novel. Mirisch wasted no time in putting the production on a fast track. On March 25, he signed William Cameron Menzies to direct the movie. Menzies, who had recently finished directing *Invaders from Mars* for 20th Century Fox, was intrigued by Dali's uncanny images within his artwork and believed that he could fashion an interesting movie around them. However, by the time filming began, Dali's artwork was no longer part of the deal. Filming began on April 20 and was completed on May 4. (Above information courtesy of the 3D Film Archive website.)

Allied Artists' film version of *The Maze* follows the plot of the novel fairly closely, though with significant changes. In fact, Dan Ullman's screenplay improves upon the novel in some respects. Kitty assumes a more prominent

STUDIO news FLASHES

3-D MOVIE UNLOCKS BAFFLING MYSTERY

HOLLYWOOD—The first great suspense novel to be filmed in third dimension is ready to thrill theatre audiences. "The Maze," large-scale Allied Artists production, was adapted from the gripping mystery classic by Maurice Sandoz. It stars Richard Carlson and Veronica Hurst, the latter a flaxen-haired European screen star brought to Hollywood for this movie.

FRANTIC LOVERS CAUGHT IN MAZE

A mystifying web of fate and an actual hedge-trap that threatens extinction to anyone caught in it keep spectators on edge during showing of "The Maze." Richard Carlson and Veronica Hurst here cling to each other as evil forces close in on them.

Bare-Legged Beauty, Strange Monster Leap Into Audience From 3-D Screen!

A moment after you witness this balancing feat in a night-club scene in "The Maze," you will gasp as the girl in tights leaps out from the screen, seemingly right into your lap. Filmed entirely in third dimension, "The Maze" gives theatre audiences the feeling of being part of the story unfolded on the screen.

Patrons are asked not to reveal the terrifying secret that hovers over the lives of men and women brought together by strange destiny in "The Maze." The exposé of the secret startles audiences of the amazing 3-D movie.

ALLIED ARTISTS presents "The MAZE" starring RICHARD CARLSON • VERONICA HURST with Katherine Emery • Michael Pate • Hillary Brooke **IN 3-DIMENSIONS**

---

role, Harry Seymour is eliminated, new characters are introduced and the time period is condensed. The movie begins with the discovery of the death of the current baronet of Craven Castle by his two servants, William and Robert. Edith Murray then addresses the camera and narrates the story which begins on the French Riviera where she and Kitty are vacationing with Kitty's fiancé, Gerald MacTeam. Gerald is the nephew of the deceased baronet and is next in line to succeed him. Upon being summoned to Craven, Gerald promises to

Gerald and his guests look up toward the castle's walls as the frog appears at a window.

return in time for his wedding two weeks later. However, shortly thereafter he writes and breaks off his engagement. Puzzled and hurt, Kitty convinces Edith to travel with her to Craven Castle. When they arrive at the castle without an invitation, Gerald responds with hostility. This creates tension between the film's characters that the novel lacks.

Kitty is shocked at Gerald's changed appearance and is hurt by his demand that she and Edith immediately leave. Kitty and Edith are also puzzled by the fact that the servants lock their rooms at night. But Kitty is determined to help Gerald, despite his resentment. Discovering a secret window that overlooks the maze next to the castle, she observes strange lights and murky processions moving toward the center of the maze. Within the castle, she also discovers strangely shaped, moist prints on the stairway which has abnormally protracted steps. Worried about Gerald's mental state, Kitty secretly invites a doctor and other friends to the castle. (This development from screenwriter Ullman is more logical than the events of the novel in which it seems unlikely that Gerald would invite friends for a grouse hunt because of the castle's secret.) The appearance of the new visitors infuriates Gerald who seemingly is becoming increasingly unbalanced by some unknown stress in addition to his unwanted guests. Meanwhile, Edith locates a library but with no furniture and very low

The tragic creature with the body of a frog and the mind of a man

shelves. More alarmingly, she gets a glimpse of a strange creature in the darkness before it scurries away. One night, Kitty is able to steal a key to their locked room and ventures out with Edith to explore the maze. After they become separated, they both encounter the same terrifying creature, an enormous frog-like beast. As in the novel, the same death in the family occurs though under dramatically different circumstances but is followed by a similar happy ending with a poignant coda.

What is the secret of Craven Castle? To answer that question, it is necessary to return in time to the 18th century and to introduce the story's protagonist who will undergo unbelievable emotional torment through no fault of his own. The year is 1750 and the Baronet and Baroness of Craven Castle are overjoyed as they await the birth of their first child. But their joy soon turns to horror as the Baroness gives birth to a freak of nature that appears to resemble a frog. The Baroness dies soon thereafter but the creature survives with the body of a frog and the mind of a man. He is christened Roger Philip MacTeam and is the rightful heir to the estate. As his size increases, he develops the intellect of a man. The Baronets of each generation keep him hidden away from everyone except the loyal servants who assume responsibility for his needs, including his

William (Michael Pate) reluctantly allows Kitty (Veronica Hurst) and Edith (Katherine Emery) to enter the castle.

education for which they assemble a special library. And thus the secret of Craven Castle passes down from generation to generation, from uncle to nephew. Since frogs have lifespans that exceed those of humans, Roger survives multiple generations and remains the true Baronet of Craven Castle.

It is difficult to imagine the horror that Roger must have endured decade after decade. If he had not developed mentally and intellectually as a man, then he could well have tolerated his existence as a frog. But he was denied such a blessing. He was cursed with having the intellect of a man but being imprisoned within the body of a gigantic frog. He had sufficient human emotions to know that he was so hideous that normal humans fainted or ran in terror upon sighting him. He was able to read books but was unable to share his thoughts with any other being. He had the ability to understand human language but could only emit partially guttural sounds which the servants learned to decipher. He had the vulnerability to elicit sympathy and even fondness from servants, all of whom he outlived. He had enough intelligence to know that he was such a burden that it drove baronets to early deaths. One of his few pleasures was when the servants took him out nightly to the freshwater pond in the center of the maze to swim in his natural environment. But he was devoid of human companionship as well as amphibian companionship because he didn't fit into either form of life.

Sir Roger Philip MacTeam, Baronet of Craven Castle.

Roger Philip MacTeam is a tragic creature due not only to the suffering he endured but also to the fact that hidden within his heart was an innate gentleness. He didn't intend to frighten Edith or Kitty, though he understood their reaction. Upon causing them such fright, he hastened away in panic as fast as he could. Now the question is whether he accidentally fell to his death or did he deliberately throw himself from the window? Did the shock of seeing human females remind him of the kind of love that he had read about but could never experience? Was this the last straw that drove him to suicide? Or did he in his own panic accidentally plunge to his death? These questions are left unanswered. What is clear is the fact that he endured the horror of being trapped within a monstrous body for more than two centuries. This is what makes *The Maze* a genuine and unique horror movie. So many of today's cynical critics and viewers who scoff at the primitive appearance of the creature cannot comprehend this obvious fact; being accustomed to computerized state-of-the-art special effects, they can only enjoy surface horrors and are incapable of discerning subliminal horrors.

In the movie's epilogue, Gerald explains the sad history of his ancestor. According to zoologist and evolutionist Ernst Haekel's (1834-1919) now-discredited theory of recapitulation, or biogenic law, the human embryo passes through all stages of evolution, from invertebrate to amphibian to reptile to mammal. Somehow, Roger became stuck in the amphibian stage in the embryo and never evolved to the human stage. So he was cursed to spend his unnatural existence as half-man and half-frog. As each nephew assumed the nominal title of baronet, the servants informed him of the family secret and this knowledge, along with the ensuing responsibility, prematurely aged him. But Roger was still officially the Lord of the Castle and was treated as such until his death 203 years after his birth.

The movie's conclusion is more logical than that of the novel. In the novel, Roger dies of congestion, a diagnosis from the court physician whom Gerald has summoned to the castle. It seems overly contrived that he should die of an illness at the same time that Edith is at the castle trying to solve the mystery. In the movie, Roger dies—whether by accident or suicide—as a direct result of the appearance at the castle, and more specifically within the maze, of Kitty and Edith. There is nothing contrived about this, and it is a far more plausible development. Incidentally, upon Roger's death in the novel, Gerald is relieved and happy that he can now resume an ordinary life and marry Kitty. In the movie, he appears relieved but is also sorrowful to some degree, making him perhaps more compassionate than his novel's counterpart. Such compassion is

Gerald (Richard Carlson) kneels by the lifeless body of the frog; Robert (Stanley Fraser), Kitty (Veronica Hurst), Dr. Dilling (John Dodsworth) and William (Michael Pate) are behind him.

William Cameron Menzies

understandable because, as the servants mourn, they fondly referred to Roger as 'The Old Gentlemen,' which is what he indeed was—in his heart if not in his body.

Such a bizarre story required a unique director to bring it to the screen. William Cameron Menzies has been justly celebrated as the most innovative and influential Art Director in Hollywood history. His contribution to any film that he worked on extended beyond art direction due to his meticulous and voluminous production drawings which contributed immeasurably to the overall look of a film. Indeed, David O. Selznick created the title of Production Designer for him because of his extensive work on *Gone with the Wind*, for which he received his second Academy Award. His work on both versions of *The Thief of Bagdad* (1924 and 1940) influenced every Arabian Nights movie that followed and proved his expertise with fantastic subjects. He was also a director, though he was less acclaimed in that field. Because his designs could often be so fanciful, his resumé included some science fiction movies. His first movie as a director was *Things to Come* (1937), based upon the novel *The Shape of Things to Come* by H.G. Wells. *The Whip Hand* (1951) contains some science fictional elements but is more of a thriller (and a confused one at that since RKO studio chief Howard Hughes changed the entire concept of the movie after Menzies had completed filming). Undoubtedly his most famous science fiction movie is *Invaders from Mars* which 20th Century Fox released just two months prior to *The Maze*.

Some enthusiasts of Menzies feel that *The Maze* is one of the least impressive of the movies that he directed, perhaps in part because it was filmed on Allied Artists' studio sets. Furthermore, almost the entire movie takes place within the castle and in the nearby maze. In his biography of Menzies, *The Shape of Films to Come* (Pantheon Books; 2015), James Curtis devotes less than a single page to *The Maze* and criticizes, among other things,

Edith (Katherine Emery) and Kitty explore the castle after stealing a key.

Italian poster for *The Maze*

The mysterious maze that is adjacent to the castle.

its "talky script" and its "plain and unimaginative sets." Curtis doesn't blame Menzies for these deficiencies. He writes that after the producers eliminated Salvador Dali's conceptions, Menzies was left with little time to prepare for the production. Curtis writes: "Unable to influence the overall look of the film, Menzies was left to thumbnail the visual effects and make an occasional embellishment; without an overall design concept, the effects tended to be gimmicks."

In actuality, the movie is quite notable. Menzies' familiar use of shadows and lighting generate an ominous atmosphere in both the castle and in the maze. His design of Craven Castle is particularly impressive with its foreboding exterior and its dark, oppressive interiors. Indeed, it is difficult to believe that this is not an actual castle in North Scotland. The maze is also quite imposing as well as unnerving with the studio props looking exactly like they are actual yew trees that were planted hundreds of years earlier. Although the film only depicts a few of the passageways within the maze, the director's imaginative set design suggests vast entwined passages beyond those that are depicted. Menzies may have been working under pressure and with limited resources, but his innate skill still shines through.

The intricacy of the maze is enhanced by the use of the three-dimensional cameras. While Menzies provides the expected gimmicks of a 3-D film, resulting in everything from bats and cobwebs to an envelope and even a dancer popping out of the screen, it is his use of depth for the intricate maze as well as the castle interiors that is most successful. However, he also knew that many theaters would show the movie in its "flat" version, so he was careful not to make the three-dimensional shots essential to the storyline. Like the best 3-D films of the 1950s (*Hondo, Dial M for Murder, Inferno,* etc.), viewers can appreciate *The Maze* in the traditional two dimensions because Menzies knows how to build and sustain a mood of suspense. While it is true that Menzies' imaginative use of the third dimension is missing from the flat version, the story still has enough power to maintain audience interest. As the mystery unfolds, the tension gradually builds to its conclusion which is as horrifying in 2-D as it is in 3-D. The appearance of the giant frog is certainly frightening in itself but its pathos will only be revealed later. Herein lies the ultimate success of the film because, despite the shocking denouement, Menzies is then able to engage the audience emotionally as Gerald provides Roger's tragic history.

Walter Mirisch had hoped that producing the movie in 3-D would acquire bookings in first-class theaters in major cities and the strategy worked. In Los Angeles, *The Maze* opened on July 2 in both the Hollywood and Downtown Paramount Theaters where it was accompanied by two 3-D shorts, *College Capers* and *Doom Town*; *Variety* reported a first week take of an "excellent $35,000." In New York City, it opened along with eight vaude-

ville acts at the Palace Theater where it earned "a rousing $25,000." Allied Artists was pleased with these initial results and announced plans for four additional 3-D movies. However, grosses were less impressive across the country. In Boston, it opened to a "nice $5,000" while Seattle registered a "fair $7,000" and Detroit reported a "poor $6,000."

It should be noted that *The Maze* was competing in many cities with several other 3-D movies. Also, due to a shortage of theaters equipped to show 3-D movies, it played in its 2-D version in smaller venues and the box-office take was at best mediocre. As a result, the movie didn't earn a place on *Variety*'s year-end list of top-grossing movies. Consequently, *The Maze* would be AA's only 3-D theatrical release; AA filmed *Dragonfly Squadron* in 3-D but released it in 2-D. In his book, *I Thought We Were Making Movies, Not History* (University of Wisconsin Press; 2008), Walter Mirisch writes: "By the time we finished the movie, the 3-D craze had petered out and the picture was not successful, either artistically or commercially." However, other factors must have played a part in the movie's commercial fate. One hundred thirty-five movies qualify for inclusion on *Variety*'s list and these include 12 3-D movies out of the 28 that Hollywood released throughout the year. *House of Wax*, which was filmed in less than a month and released in April is seventh on the list and the Western, *The Charge at Feather River*, released in June, is 12th. Other 3-D movies earning positions on the list were the adventure film, *Second Chance*, and the musical, *Kiss Me Kate*, both of which were released later in the year. *It Came from Outer Space* (science fiction), *Fort Ti* (Western) and *Sangaree* (adventure) were competing with *The Maze* for 3-D playdates in June and were also profitable enough to earn positions on the list. So 3-D movies were still lucrative toward the end of 1953. However, 20th Century Fox's re-

Richard Carlson and Veronica Hurst pose for a publicity photo.

lease in September of *The Robe*, the first Cinemascope feature, signified the eventual demise of 3-D movies. It is significant that Fox advertised Cinemascope as "The Modern Miracle You See Without Glasses." *The Robe* was the highest-grossing movie of the year and earned more than all of the 3-D movies combined. The following year, Hollywood released fifteen 3-D movies but the writing was on the wall for the so-called depthies.

The box-office disappointment of *The Maze* does not reflect its quality. Phil Hardy in *Science Fiction: The Film Encyclopedia* (William Morrow; 1984) calls it "a highly original, flawed piece (and) a very strange, grotesquely fascinating movie, competently directed by Menzies and full of suspense, yet almost ruined by a small budget." In *The Great Science Fiction Pictures II* (Scarecrow Press; 1990), James Robert Parrish and Michael R. Pitts call it "an engrossing minor sci-fi film, relying more on pathos than thrills." Bill Warren in *Keep Watching the Skies* (McFarland; 1982) writes: "This is one of the damnedest films ever made; for those with an exotic sense of sympathy the ending of this rather grotesque little film can be surprisingly moving." Jeff Rovin in *Those Fabulous Fantasy Films* (A.S. Barnes; 1977) writes: "It is the striking

Kitty hears strange sounds outside her door in the middle of the night.

sets and photography that are the movie's real star." John Baxter in *Science Fiction in the Cinema* (Paperback Library; 1970) writes: "This is a clever piece of horror/sf; the maze is an ideal setting for 3-D effects and even projected in 2-D the images have a remarkable depth; the castle with trees like black spiders, huge doors and odd ramp-like stairs leading to a forbidden chamber is a splendid creation."

The actors are all more than competent. Richard Carlson starred in several science fiction movies in the 1950s, including *It Came from Outer Space* (1953) and *Creature from the Black Lagoon* (1954), both in 3-D. He also starred in *Magnetic Monster* (1953) which Curt Siodmak wrote and co-directed. He was a prolific director as well; he directed and co-starred in *Riders to the Stars* (1954) from a Curt Siodmak screenplay. Regardless of how fantastic the subject matter, Carlson always projected sincerity in his performances and consistently gave the impression that he genuinely believed in his characters. His portrayal of Gerald MacTeam conveys this same type of earnestness. He is totally convincing as the happy and carefree groom-to-be and as the angry, distressed lord of the castle. His intensity definitely helps to make the fantastic proceedings credible.

Veronica Hurst was imported from England to play Kitty and believably displays initial vulnerability and later pluckiness; this was her first starring role and she aquits herself quite charmingly. Katherine Emery is equally fine as Edith; she had a more successful career on Broadway and only made a dozen movies before retiring from acting after playing Edith Murray. All of the supporting actors, including such familiar names as Hillary Brooke and Michael Pate, contribute to the effectiveness of the movie by giving unaffected performances.

Following its release, *The Maze* disappeared into obscurity where it remained for several decades—but not forever. In 2018, the 3-D Film Archive in collaboration with The Film Foundation, Martin Scorsese and Paramount Pictures Archives digitally restored *The Maze* from the original left and right eye camera negatives. In August 2018, *The American Cinematheque* in Los Angeles presented the restored film at The Aero Theater in Los Angeles to an enthusiastic audience. That same month, The Film Forum Theater in New York City also exhibited the movie; Robert Furmanek, the founder of the 3-D Film Archive, introduced the movie to an equally appreciative audience. The restoration highlights Menzies' unique visual style and tends to belie reports that he had little input into the film's design. From the first shot of the door into the maze that opens to reveal a remarkable sense of depth, it is obvious that the director planned each sequence very carefully. His placement of the characters in the group scenes reveals his understanding of the psychological interaction developing within the story's development. Several impressive 3-D effects, including one breathtaking exterior shot with a tree in the foreground, reveals that he must have invested time and effort into the 3-D process. If Walter Mirisch had the opportunity to see this new restoration, he might have had to change his opinion about Menzies' artistry.

The Maze has its share of horror, science fiction, mystery and thrills. But most of all it features a truly sad ending. The closing scene of the movie begins with Edith's happy announcement of the marriage of Gerald and Kitty and their permanent residence in Craven Castle which is now free of the curse. But then Edith remembers the tragedy that is the basis of her story. As she mentions the grave that now lies in the center of the maze, the camera closes in on the headstone. It states quite simply:

Here Lies Sir Roger Phillip MacTeam, Baronet of Craven; 1750—1953.

Credits: Executive Producer: Walter Mirisch; Producer: Richard Heermance; Director and Production Designer: William Cameron Menzies; Screenplay: Dan Ullman, based upon the novel by Maurice Sandoz; Editor: John Fuller; Cinematography: Harry Neumann; Music: Marlin Skiles; Special Effects: Augie Lohman; Art Direction: David Milton; Set Decoration: Robert Priestley

Cast: Richard Carlson (Gerald MacTeam); Veronica Hurst (Kitty Murray); Katherine Emery (Edith Murray); John Dodsworth (Dr. Bert Dilling); Hillary Brooke (Peggy Lord); Michael Pate (William); Stanley Fraser (Robert); Lillian Bond (Margaret Dilling); Owen McGiveney (Simon); Robin Hughes (Richard); Clyde Cook (Cab Driver); The Phelans (Dancers)

Donovan's Brain

There is something inherently repellant about a disembodied brain surrounded by vaporous fluid in a fish tank, connected by electrodes and pulsating repeatedly—especially the way that the 1953 movie, *Donovan's Brain*, depicts it.

Curt Siodmak's novel, *Donovan's Brain*, has had many incarnations. Upon its publication in 1942, it became an immediate best-seller. In 1943, the first of three official film adaptations, entitled *The Lady and the Monster* starring Erich von Stroheim, was released. In 1944, the radio series *Suspense* broadcast a two-part adaptation of the novel with Orson Welles. In 1948, *Suspense* presented another radio adaptation with John McIntire. In 1953, the second film version, this time titled *Donovan's Brain* and starring Lew Ayres, was released. In 1955, the television anthology series *Studio One* adapted the novel with Wendell Corey. In 1962, a British-German movie adaptation titled *The Brain* with Peter van Eyck was released. Unofficial variations of the novel's theme of a disembodied brain exerting control over human beings are too numerous to mention.

Curt Siodmak (1902-2000) was a German-born novelist, screenwriter and director. He developed his skills as a science fiction writer in his native Germany, writing stories and novels in the genre. In 1926, the first science fiction magazine, *Amazing Stories*, introduced his name to the American public by translating one of his stories into English. His futuristic novel, *FPI Does Not Reply*, published in 1930, is the only one of his German novels to be translated into English. The novel was the basis for the German film, *FPI Does Not Answer* (1932), which was simultaneously filmed in English and French versions. Siodmak began his film career in his native Germany, continued it in England and journeyed to Hollywood in 1937. After Universal hired him, he received his first official credit for co-writing *The Invisible Man Returns* (1940). The movie's success paved the way for additional assignments in the science fiction and horror genres, including his most famous creation, *The Wolf Man* (1941).

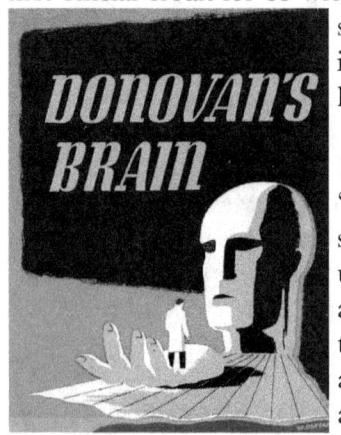

Curt Siodmak's novel

In *The Science Fiction Encyclopedia* (Doubleday; 1979), Peter Nicholls and John Brosnan write: "Siodmak has often been involved with sf-oriented subjects but has never displayed much feeling or understanding of the genre. He is obviously more at home with the supernatural, the macabre and the grotesque than with science and such science as he introduces tends to be for the picturesque atmosphere rather than for the sake of rationality or logic." Despite the accuracy of this assessment, the 1953 film version of *Donovan's Brain* qualifies as both science fiction and horror, as the novel does.

In his autobiography, *Wolf Man's Maker* (Scarecrow; 2001), Siodmak describes his situation after he was fired from *Son of Dracula*: "I didn't wait for my agent to peddle me around to find employment for me. I was going back to my original profession: writing novels. I already had the idea for *Donovan's Brain*." This would be his first novel in English. After his brother Robert began to offer unwelcome suggestions, Curt's wife arranged for him to leave Hollywood and live in a bungalow at a spa in the Mojave Desert where he proceeded to write continuously for several weeks until he completed the novel away from his brother's advice. He writes: "That novel influenced my future profession and now, 50 years after its first printing, is still reissued perennially not only here but in many other countries."

The novel unfolds through Dr. Patrick Cory's entries in his diary. The setting is a small town in the Arizona desert. Cory conducts experiments on animal brains to see if he can preserve brain tissue after death. When a private plane crashes in the nearby mountains, authorities call him to the scene after his friend, the local physician Dr. Frank Schratt, is unable to respond due to intoxication. He finds only one survivor, millionaire Warren Horace Donovan. Since there is no chance of saving the man's life, Cory illegally removes his brain and succeeds in keeping it alive. But the brain telepathically begins to exert its control over him. Cory soon learns that Donovan was a sadistic, avaricious egomaniac who delighted in controlling everyone, including his wife, son and daughter. The brain directs Cory to continue his fraudulent financial schemes and to initiate plans to free a sadistic murderer. The novel gradually builds in horror as Cory comes close to murdering his wife as well as Schratt. Cory is able to escape from the brain but only due to the heroic efforts of Schratt who sacrifices his own life to kill the brain.

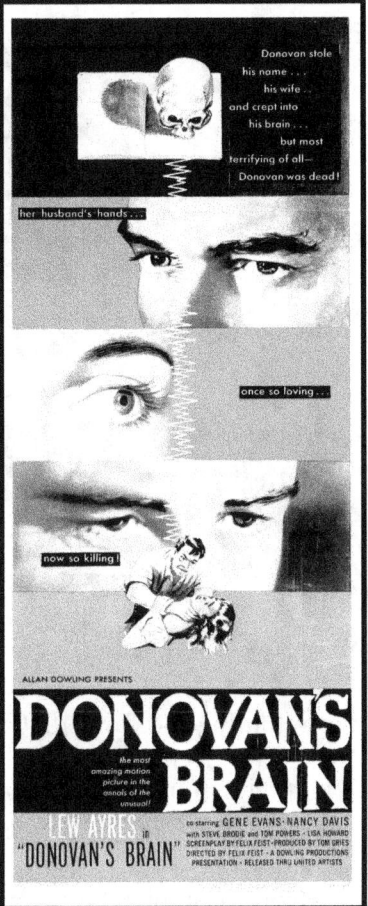

Because of the novel's worldwide popularity, a motion picture adaptation seemed almost a certainty. Since Siodmak was working at Universal at the time of the novel's publication, it seems strange that the studio didn't purchase the novel. More than any other studio, Universal was well-known for its horror

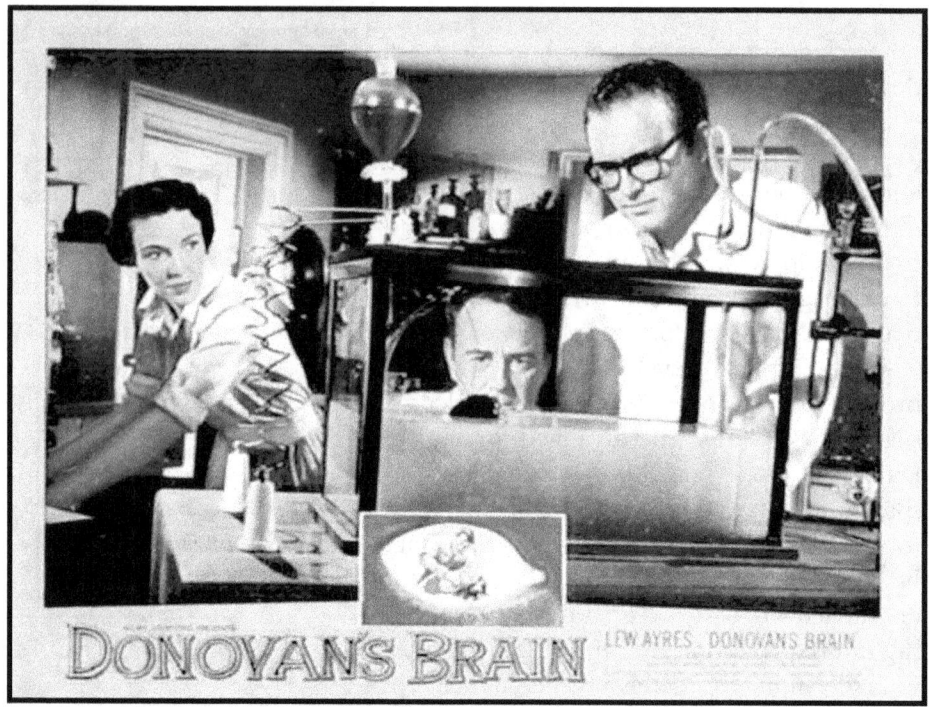

movies during the early 1940s and *Donovan's Brain* was the type of story that would have been an ideal candidate for the studio's recognizable style, especially if the author could have written the screenplay. For whatever reason, Universal passed on the project and second-tier Republic Pictures snapped up the film rights.

Republic studio chief Herbert J. Yates used the novel as a vehicle for his future wife, Vera Hruba Ralston. Though the novel's title was familiar to the public, Republic titled its film version *The Lady and the Monster*, which gives an indication of the movie's low ambitions. A gothic-type castle replaces Cory's home as the setting and a new character is added. Erich von Stroheim plays Professor Franz Mueller, a deranged scientist who preserves the brain of dead millionaire Donovan. This allows Dr. Cory, played by Richard Arlen, to be a hero as well as a victim while Mueller assumes the negative characteristics of the novel's Cory. Ralston plays Cory's girlfriend whom Mueller covets. Events eventually reveal that Donovan committed murder among his many crimes. The movie is undistinguished and unworthy of its literary origin.

It was only nine years later that the second film version premiered and this 1953 movie, entitled *Donovan's Brain*, proved to be a faithful and engrossing adaptation of the novel. United Artists released the independently-produced movie from Allan Dowling productions. It was filmed economically at Motion Picture Center Studios in Hollywood with brief location filming at the Sheraton-Town House in Los Angeles. Production began in early February and ended within the month. Allan Dowling, the presenter of the movie, had a successful career in many fields. In addition to being an occasional film producer, Dowling was an author, a poet, a librettist, a publisher and a philanthropist. He produced one other movie, a documentary entitled *Hunters of the Deep*, and presented one other movie, a romantic drama, *This Is My Love* (1954). Tom Gries, the producer of *Donovan's Brain*, began his directing career the following year and directed numerous episodes of television series as well as many theatrical movies, including *Will Penny* (1967) and *The Hawaiians* (1970). He received three nominations from the Directors Guild of America for Outstanding Directorial Achievement in Movies for Television, including *Helter Skelter* (1976).

Felix Feist directed and wrote the screenplay for *Donovan's Brain*. Throughout his career, Feist wasn't known for any individual directorial touches, but he was efficient and consistently displayed a knack for storytelling. He began his directing career with a spectacular science fiction/disaster movie, *Deluge* (1932) and then directed shorts for the next decade before returning to feature films. His next movies were of varying quality and included westerns, comedies and sports films as well as some film noirs, such as *The Devil Thumbs a Ride* (1947) and *The Man Who Cheated Himself* (1950). He returned to the science fiction genre with *Donovan's Brain* and, for the most part, his direction is straightforward. The movie is in black-and-white, which allows him to inject some noirish touches that befits the theme of a good man being corrupted by his own ambition as well as an external evil. This includes the use of light and shadows to enhance the impact of the brain's power. The movie contains little action

The brain of W.H. Donovan begins to exert control over Dr. Patrick Cory (Lew Ayres).

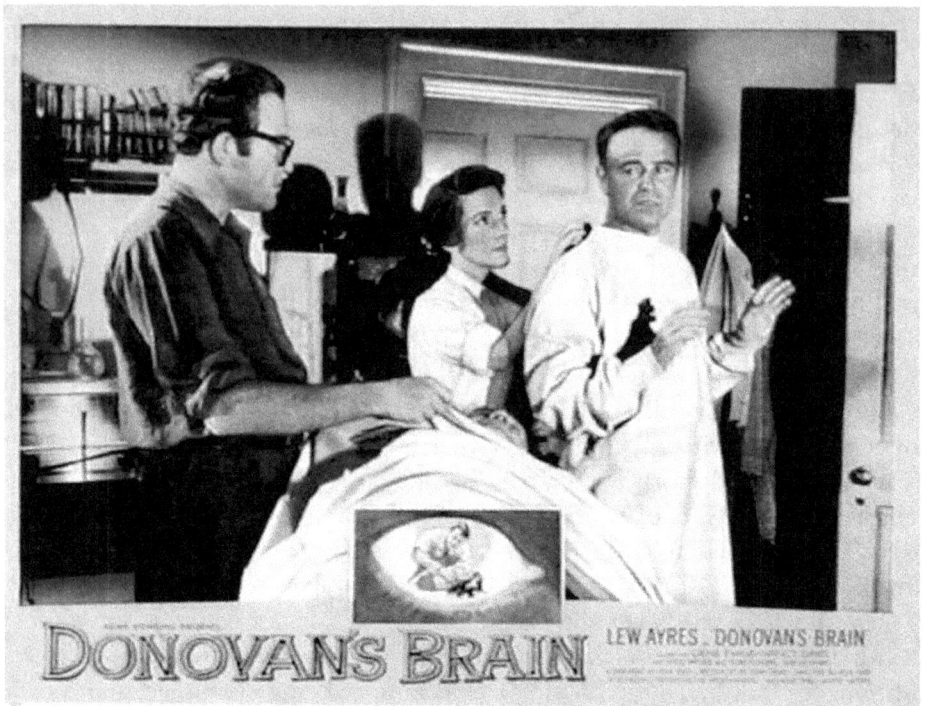

Cory, assisted by Dr. Schratt (Gene Evans) and wife Janice (Nancy Davis), prepares to operate on Donovan to try to save his life.

but maintains interest through personal conflicts and builds suspense from its theme of implicit horror.

The plot follows the novel fairly closely. Dr. Patrick Cory arrives at the scene of an airplane crash, discovers the dying millionaire W. H. Donovan, transports him back to his laboratory and eventually removes the brain from the dead man's body. His friend and fellow doctor, the alcoholic Dr. Schratt, warns him against such an illegal as well as ungodly procedure but Cory persists and is able to keep the brain alive. When he succeeds in telepathically communicating with the brain, this proves to be his second mistake. Soon the brain is controlling him, directing him and ordering him to commit nefarious acts. But Cory doesn't just obey orders. He gradually assumes the dead man's habits, mannerisms and characteristics; he walks with a limp, smokes expensive cigars, wears custom-made suits and treats people contemptuously. A blackmailing reporter named Yokum causes problems for Cory but only until he comes into close contact with the brain. Donovan's son and daughter, who despised him for good reason, become his victims again when Cory inflicts their father's punishment upon them. Nothing seems to be able to control the brain's evil as it gradually occupies Cory's brain. However, the brain has one defect; it can only concentrate on a single thought at a time. This allows Schratt to try to kill the brain while Janice (Cory's wife) distracts Cory, but he proves to be ineffective. In a moment of lucidity, Cory gives Janice specific instructions (which viewers do not hear) on a ploy that eventually succeeds and saves Cory just before the brain completely subjugates his mind.

Feists' screenplay, from an adaptation by Hugh Brooke, makes some changes to the story. In the novel, Cory is an arrogant and unethical scientist who is inconsiderate of his wife and of Schratt. In the film, Cory is a noble researcher who loves his wife and protects Dr. Schratt. This makes his eventual transformation into the evil Donovan more shocking, especially as he becomes increasingly cruel and devious. To some degree, the movie proceeds as a cautionary tale about the dangers of excessive scientific technology. It includes debates about science encroaching on God's will but with subtle implications. For instance, Schratt tells Cory that removing the brain is sacrilegious, but Cory affirms that his medical skills came from God, implying that his actions are God's will. Lightning eventually destroys the brain, an act which on the surface seems to emanate from the heavens. But then viewers learn that Cory's instructions to Janice directed her to reroute their home's lightning rod so that it would electrocute the brain. Thus, the film's message is not as simplistic as it may seem.

One of the intriguing elements of the movie is the manner in which Donovan's brain exploits Cory's altruism, specifically concerning his desire to

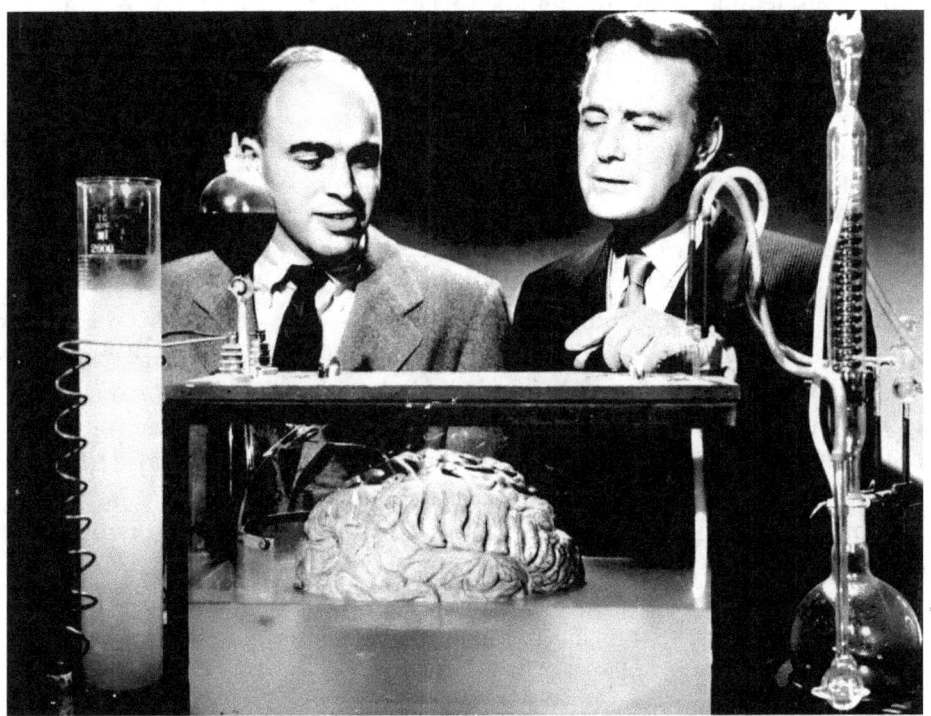

Tom Gries, the movie's producer, and Lew Ayres appear to be marveling at the realism of the brain.

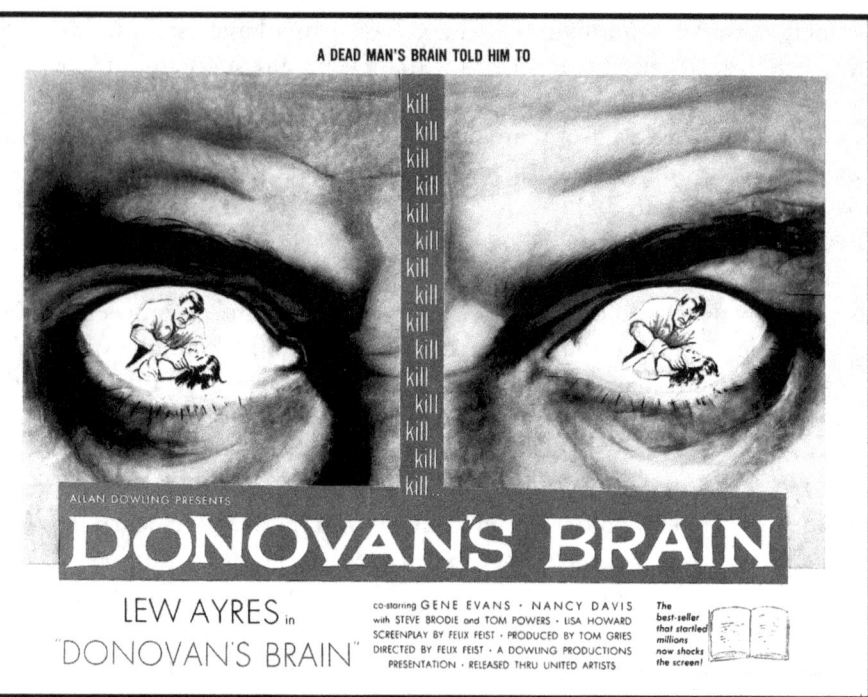

achieve a scientific breakthrough for the benefit of humanity. The disembodied brain knows how to manipulate Cory by giving him access to Donovan's wealth, supposedly for beneficial purposes. Though Cory's motivations are initially humane, his subsequent inhumane actions have made him susceptible to the brain's calculations. Consequently, the transformed doctor uses the wealth for Donovan's ends and not his own. He gradually relinquishes his mind to the conniving thoughts of the living brain. Cory, initially a sympathetic protagonist, becomes a merciless antagonist. Dr. Patrick Cory, in effect, becomes Warren Horace Donovan. Fortunately, he had a loyal friend and a loyal wife who save him from total abdication of his mind.

Regarding the movie's epilogue, some of the movie's scoffers complain that Cory gets off too leniently, in view of the damage that his experiment caused, including Yokum's death; in the novel, Yokum and Schratt both die, but in the movie Schratt survives the brain's attempts to kill him. However, authorities do take him away and it is implied that he will pay for his crimes and may have to go to prison. In the novel, Cory doesn't face any legal repercussions and, after a lengthy stay in the hospital to repair his damaged brain, he intends to take over Schratt's position as county physician. He does write rather humbly that he has learned from his experiment: "Nature has set limits that man cannot pass."

The starring performance of Lew Ayres is one of the primary reasons that *Donovan's Brain* makes such an impact. Ayres had been acting for over two decades and had been a major star since receiving acclaim for *All Quiet on the Western Front* (1932). He later achieved great popularity for playing Dr. Kildare in a series of popular movies from 1938 to 1942. In 1949, his role in *Johnny Belinda* earned him a Best Actor Academy Award nomination. *Donovan's Brain* was his first science fiction movie. As Dr. Patrick Cory, he delivers an exceptional performance and instills him with an innate sense of dignity. He expertly projects the diverse nuances of his character and portrays a man who is overly confident in his own abilities but becomes increasingly conflicted as he gradually recognizes the dangers of his experiment. What is extraordinary about his portrayal is that he conveys Cory's transformation into Donovan with absolutely no make-up or any other accoutrements that usually accompany such alterations. He hardens his features, narrows his eyes, purses his lips and visibly seems to become a different person. It is truly a marvelous performance.

Gene Evans is fine as Schratt, frequently seeming to be just on the border of sobriety, while Nancy Davis suitably projects Janice's selfless devotion. Steve Bodie instills reporter Yokum with just the right amount of sleaziness. All of the supporting performances are quite fine, but the movie belongs to Lew Ayres. However, his performance and the movie were largely ignored. And of the few critics who reviewed it, some thought they were being witty by

Cory shows Schratt and Janice that the signature he wrote under the control of the disembodied brain is the same as Donovan's signature.

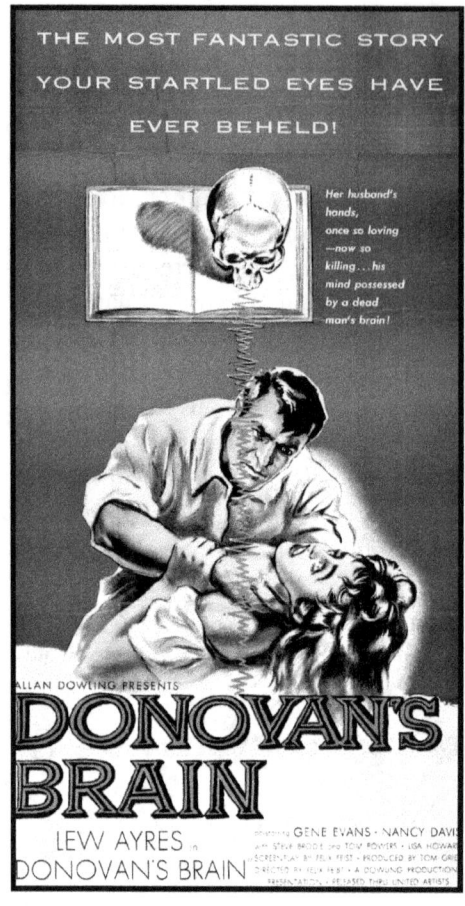

writing that Dr. Kildare would have his medical license revoked if he did what Dr. Cory does. Many people invested time and effort into the making of *Donovan's Brain* and they probably realized that negative criticism of the finished product was always a possibility. But when critics use their movie as the punchline of a joke, it is really aggravating, especially when the joke is so banal.

At least *Variety* gave *Donovan's Brain* a positive review: "This is a well-made science fiction horror feature that is grim stuff put together in a more polished fashion than most such horror entries; Tom Gries' production guidance is well-valued, achieving effects beyond its budget." Unfortunately, due to the timing of its release, the movie faced a handicap from the beginning. United Artists released it one week after *The Robe* premiered and was breaking all box-office records. A small black-and-white movie on a normal-sized screen seemed quaint compared to the luxurious Cinemascope Technicolor film with Stereophonic Sound.

In some areas, *Donovan's Brain* opened as a single feature, but reviews were not encouraging. For instance, upon its New York City opening, Bosley Crowther in *The New York Times* wrote: "The whole thing is utterly silly." It did only fair business and closed quickly. In Portland, it was again a single feature, but *Variety* describes its box-office as "dull." In other cities it opened as part of a double bill with UA programmers such as *Shark River* and *Go Man Go* but the box-office didn't improve. By the time it reached smaller venues, it was the supporting feature to more successful movies from UA and from other studios. Consequently, it didn't earn the minimum of $1,000,000 in domestic theatrical rentals to qualify for inclusion on *Variety*'s list of Top Grossing Movies of the year.

Just for the record, almost two decades later, the 1962 film version of the novel, entitled *The Brain* (aka *Vengeance*) was released. Though it follows the novel's plot fairly closely in the beginning, it becomes a detective story as the disembodied brain directs Dr. Corrie (sic) to find out who caused the plane crash and murdered him. Peter Van Eyck stars as Corrie with Anne Heywood as his romantic interest. A company called Governor Films released the movie in the United States where it attracted little attention.

Felix Feist directed only one more theatrical movie after *Donovan's Brain* and then spent the remainder of his career in television as producer and writer as well as director; his future credits include directing episodes of the science fiction series, *Voyage to the Bottom of the Sea* and *The Outer Limits*. Lew Ayres continued to act for another four decades and appeared in the science fiction sequel, *Battle for the Planet of the Apes* (1975), the horror sequel, *Damien: Omen 2* (1978) and the horror television movie, *Salem's Lot* (1979). Interestingly, though Curt Siodmak was a successful screenwriter, he was not asked to write the screenplay for any of the film versions of *Donovan's Brain*. And while he began his directing career with a low budget B movie called *Bride of the Gorilla* (1951), he didn't have the opportunity to direct the 1953 film version of his novel. However, that same year, he wrote and directed *Magnetic Monster* which has developed a cult following; according to some reports, an uncredited Herbert Strock co-directed the movie. By the way, two of his later novels, *Hauser's Memory* and *Gabriel's Body*, feature Dr. Patrick Cory, but neither repeated the tremendous success of the earlier novel.

The filmmakers of *Donovan's Brain* had modest intentions. They hoped to make a good movie from a good novel. They hoped to make a movie that would entertain audiences for perhaps an hour and a half and hopefully even earn a profit. *Donovan's Brain* may have been a failure at the box-office, but it definitely succeeds in being entertaining. And it is certainly deliberate that, since the movie is about a brain, it stimulates the brains of viewers.

However, *Donovan's Brain* also contains an enduring legacy. The haunting image of that throbbing, hideous, disembodied brain left a lasting impression upon untold numbers of moviegoers. Creating such an indelible a memory is quite an achievement for any movie. This makes the movie an indisputable success.

Credits: Presenter/Executive Producer: Allan Dowling; Producer: Tom Gries; Director: Felix Feist; Screenplay: Felix Feist, from an adaptation by Hugh Brooke, based upon the novel by Curt Siodmak; Cinematographer: Joseph Biroc; Editor: Herbert L. Strock; Production Designer: Boris Leven; Music: Eddie Dunstedtler; Special Effects: Harry Redmond, Jr.; Set Decoration: Edward G. Boyle

Cast: Lew Ayres (Dr. Patrick Cory); Gene Evans (Dr. Frank Schratt); Nancy Davis (Janice Cory); Steve Brodie (Herbie Yokum); Tom Powers (Washington Advisor); Lisa K. Howard (Chloe Donovan); Michael Colgan (Tom Donovan); Kyle James (Chief Tuttle); Victor Sutherland (Nathaniel Fuller); Peter Adams (Webster); Harlan Warde (Brooke)

1984

George Orwell, a pseudonym of Eric Arthur Blair (1903-1950), wrote *1984*—also known as *Nineteen Eighty-Four*—in 1949 and it is a genuine literary masterpiece. Orwell was one of the most renowned authors of the 20th century. If he had written only *1984*, he would be justly celebrated but he wrote another certified classic, *Animal Farm*, in 1945. He was also a political commentator, essayist, journalist, poet and satirist. *1984* has been adapted several times for radio, three times for television, once as a play, once even as a ballet and twice for motion pictures. Columbia pictures released the first film version in 1956. Michael Anderson directed the movie, and it stars Edmond O'Brien, Michael Redgrave and Jan Sterling.

The movie has a terrible reputation which may be due in part to the fact that Orwell's estate withdrew it from circulation following the expiration of its distribution agreement. Orwell's widow, Sonia Brownell, managed the estate and reportedly disliked the movie. Most reference books agree with Brownell and denigrate it. Phil Hardy in *Science Fiction: The Film Encyclopedia* (William Morrow; 1984) dismisses it as "a simplified version of the book that pays little heed to the ideas that make it so significant a work." Bill Warren in *Keep Watching the Skies* (McFarland; 1982) writes: "The movie has no drive or energy; Edmond O'Brien is miscast (and) Michael Anderson is in his usual rut." Jeff Rovin in *A Pictorial History of Science Fiction Films* (Citadel; 1979) writes that it is "a great disappointment and a lackluster adaptation of the brilliant novel." In *The Science Fiction Encyclopedia* (Doubleday; 1979) edited by Peter Nicholls, John Brosnan calls it "an over-careful and lifeless film with a miscast Edmond O'Brien." In *The Great Science Fiction Pictures* (Scarecrow Press; 1977), James Robert Parish and Michael R. Pitts describe it as "a relatively mundane movie that depicts few of the horrors of the Orwell state." In *Things to Come: An Illustrated History of the Science Fiction Film* (Times Books; 1977), Douglas Menville and R. Reginald, a pseudonym of Michael Burgess, call it "a watered-down version of the novel." John Baxter in *Science Fiction in the Cinema* (Paperback Library; 1970) scorns it as "a failure and a boiled-down version of Orwell with an indecent accent on horror."

These critics are mistaken. To begin with, the credits of the movie state that the

screenplay is "freely adapted from the novel." Thus, the creators of the movie did not intend for it to be a complete or unqualified adaptation. In actuality, an accurate film version of the novel would require several hours to fully depict

Cover of the UK Region 2 DVD

its many philosophical and political plot threads along with its multitude of characters. Nevertheless, though the screenplay by William Templeton and Ralph Bettinson naturally condenses the novel, it captures its essence and is quite faithful to Orwell's narrative. The movie certainly doesn't deserve its dismal reputation. Indeed, Douglas Brode stands out from the crowd with his book, *Fantastic Planets, Forbidden Zones and Lost Continents* (University of Texas Press; 2015), in which he cites *1984* as one of the 100 greatest science fiction films.

Ironically, though *1984* condemns a fictional totalitarian government, the film's production reveals actual government influence. While the movie is a British production filmed completely in England, the U.S. Information Agency partially financed it to promote anti-communism. The movie is officially a Holiday Film Production, a company that produced no other movies. The producer of the film is N. Peter Rathvon; Rathvon's obituary in *The New York Times* describes him as an industrialist and a former officer of various United States corporations. This is the only movie that he personally produced; he was the executive producer of one other movie. The production and release of *1984* occurred in the midst of the Cold War when the world's two superpowers, the United States and the Soviet Union, were engaging in a continual state of conflict by utilizing politics, economics and propaganda to achieve global dominance. Propaganda was a useful weapon that both superpowers utilized through the media, including motion pictures, to promote their agendas. Because Orwell's novel warned against the evils of totalitarianism, the USIA apparently believed that a film version would be an influential device to depict the horrors of a tyrannical government similar to that of the Soviet Union.

Not coincidentally, it was George Orwell who coined the term Cold War in a 1945 article entitled "You and the Atomic Bomb" when he predicted that the future would involve two or three superstates striving for control of the world with the continual threat of nuclear annihilation creating fear and anxiety throughout the globe. This amazingly accurate prediction would be the genesis of his dystopian novel, *1984*. Though Orwell witnessed the Cold War, he didn't live to see the prevalence of many of his other predictions, including perpetual wars, revision of history, mass surveillance, loss of privacy and suppression of free speech, all of which have become commonplace by the end of the first quarter of the 21st century. It may be only a matter of time before the emergence of some form of government-decreed Newspeak with a restricted vocabulary designed to restrain each person's ability to verbalize or even think seditious thoughts which are any thoughts that contradict government ideology.

The 1956 film version of *1984* has many of the qualities of a film noir. The movie is in black-and-white with many scenes accentuating the gloomy atmosphere of the setting. In conventional film noir, the forbidden environment usually exists underground or on the fringes of regular society. But in this movie, the entire society is a noir environment in which danger literally lurks around every corner. Telescreens are in every home and workplace, denying privacy to everyone and creating a perpetual fear of being arrested for real or imaginary crimes against the state. Spies are everywhere and may include your friends, neighbors and coworkers. Police cars patrol the streets with officers who have the authority to question and remand anyone. There is no safe place, no refuge from the despotic government.

At the Hate Week rally, members of the Outer Party vigorously express their hatred for enemies of the state and their love for Big Brother.

Science Fiction Thrills...Horror Chills

Edmond O'Brien poses for a publicity photo.

Winston Smith, the movie's protagonist, possesses the qualities of a film noir hero. He is a loner and feels alienated within his society. He is disillusioned due to his government's dishonesty but feels powerless to do anything about it. He is flawed due to his fear of rats which is the result of trauma from his childhood. He feels trapped and has a fatalistic outlook about his future. His desperate longing to achieve freedom will propel him to rebellion. Unfortunately, like most noir protagonists, he never had a chance and was doomed from the beginning.

The setting of the movie is London in the futuristic year of 1984. Nuclear war in the 1960s devastated the globe and created three superstates: Oceania, Eurasia and Eastasia. London is the capital of Airstrip One, one of the largest provinces of Oceania, which is at war with Eurasia and Eastasia. Big Brother, whose ominous visage is on posters everywhere, governs Oceania. However, Big Brother is never actually seen and might be a fictitious person that the ruling powers have created to instill fear within the population. Oceana's society is divided into three classes. At the top of the social strata is the dominant Inner Party, the upper-class members who control the state and manage the government ministries. The Outer Party comprises the middle-class members who work within the ministries and are under constant surveillance by the Inner Party. The People are the lower-class uneducated masses that live in slums and perform manual labor.

The Inner Party exploits the perpetual state of warfare to convince Oceania's citizens of the necessity of protection by the state. It demands absolute conformity within the Outer Party. Men and women of the Outer Party wear similarly drab clothing to discourage any kind of prohibited intimacy. They must regularly participate in Two Minute Hate Sessions, during which they have to emotionally display their loathing for the enemy and their devotion to Big Brother. They must accept the reality of Doublethink, which coerces them into simultaneously believing two contradictory principles or concepts, including the government's slogans that War is Peace, Freedom is Slavery and Ignorance is Strength. They must also direct their animosity toward members of the Underground, revolutionaries such as Jones and Rutherford whose arrest for treason Winston has witnessed. Strict adherence to the Inner Party doctrine is compulsory. Indeed, members of the Thought Police will arrest anyone whose behavior suggests that they may be *thinking* disloyal beliefs.

In the movie's epilogue, Winston (Edmond O'Brien) has been totally indoctrinated while Julia (Jan Sterling) has been purged of all hope and happiness.

The movie begins with an air raid that forces citizens to scurry for cover as bombs explode around them. Among those racing to safety is Winston Smith, a member of the Outer Party, who works at the Ministry of Truth and whose function is to re-write history and erase anything that disproves Party doctrine. He finds shelter in a doorway and, almost immediately afterward, a woman seeks refuge with him. This is Julia, who works in the fiction department of the Ministry of Truth and whom he suspects may be a member of the Thought Police. Winston doesn't speak to her and quickly leaves when it is all clear. He rushes home to his room which contains a telescreen which continuously observes him. As part of his compulsory routine, he presents his empty briefcase to the telescreen and opens his coat to show that he is not carrying anything unlawful. But on this occasion, he has smuggled into his room an illegal diary which he will use to write forbidden thoughts against Big Brother. This is the first step of his rebellion.

Spies are everywhere and even include Selena Parsons, his neighbor's young daughter. The fact that Winston fears this child is just one of the many distressing elements of his environment. Mr. Parsons is a loyal member of the Outer Party and is proud of his daughter—until he talks in his sleep. Winston's second act of rebellion happens the next evening when, after leaving

Selena Parsons (Carol Wolveridge) practices condemning Winston as a traitor.

work, he crosses over into the People's Area. Officers question him and order him to appear before an official of the Ministry of Truth. The following day, the official who grills him commands him to undergo more stringent interrogation at the Ministry of Love, the feared agency which inflicts punishment upon suspected dissidents. But O'Connor, the Inner Party administrator who has been monitoring the questioning, cancels the order and allows Winston to leave. This apparent act of kindness is the first sign to Winston that O'Connor may be an ally against Big Brother.

Another sign that Winston is not alone occurs when Julia discloses in a secret note that she loves him. Though he is initially suspicious, Winston learns to trust her and they embark on a furtive love affair, despite the fact that the only acceptable unions are those that the state arranges. Winston and Julia appreciate the kindness of Mr. Charrington, the owner of an antique shop in the People's Area who allows them to use a room above his shop

Winston and Julia (Jan Sterling) are overjoyed when O'Connor states that he is a member of the Underground; an unidentified actor plays O'Connor's servant, Martin.

Winston and Julia conduct their affair in secret—but there are no secrets under Big Brother.

for their trysts. The lovers are able to enjoy forbidden pleasure and believe that there is a chance for additional liberties. Emboldened by their affair, Winston decides to act upon his belief that O'Connor is secretly a member of the Underground. Julia insists on going with him to O'Connor's home, an apartment of relative luxury. When O'Connor confirms that he is an ally and an enemy of Big Brother, Winston and Julia are overjoyed and have hope for the future.

Winston sobbingly grovels into the arms of O'Connor after being subjected to the horrors of Room 101.

However, brutal reality quickly shatters the freedom that Winston and Julia have briefly enjoyed. Both O'Connor and Charrington reveal themselves to be loyal Inner Party members who have been entrapping the lovers into total treason. The police arrest and imprison the couple. O'Connor then personally supervises the systematic torture of Winston, a torture that is both physical and psychological. The excruciating and unending pain eventually crushes Winston's resistance until he actually accepts Doublethink and believes that O'Connor's four fingers are really five. But that isn't the end of his ordeal. When O'Connor forces him into Room 101, a horrendous chamber filled with ravenous  rats, he betrays Julia and tearfully collapses into total submission. Julia, who has been subjected to a similarly personalized torture, emerges from her incarceration as little more than a zombie, devoid of any emotion except self-contempt for her betrayal of Winston. In contrast, Winston's regret over his betrayal of Julia is brief since he has been totally indoctrinated. In the film's last scene, Winston Smith has become a passionate supporter of Big Brother.

The movie's ending is depressing but any other ending would have been dishonest to the film's depiction of a totally repressive regime. At the producer's request, Anderson also filmed an alternate ending, one in which Winston and Julia survive the torture, continue to rebel and are killed. The British release utilized this ending, and it is probably this version that angered Orwell's widow, and with good reason since it contradicts all that has preceded it and is implausible. However, the version with the brainwashed ending is the one that is generally known today. There are signs during the course of the story that foretell this pessimistic conclusion. For instance, the expression on O'Connor's face as Winston and Julia leave his home subtly suggests his duplicity. Young Selena's staunch allegiance to the Party implies that she will report even faintly suspicious behavior to the authorities, and she has already witnessed Winston's questionable actions. And Charrington's sympathetic smile seems overly artificial.

This ending is slightly different than the finale of the novel which ends with Winston quietly shedding a grateful tear at the realization that he loves Big Brother. This is effective for the printed page, but the filmmakers may have understandably believed that a more exciting final scene would be more impactful for the screen and accordingly created the movie's conclusion with Winston vociferously shouting his devotion to Big Brother. Incidentally, Orwell's conclusion contains another even more depressing detail. In the novel, the Inner Party has decreed that Winston and Julia, though successfully indoctrinated, will be killed after an indeterminate period of time as a warning to

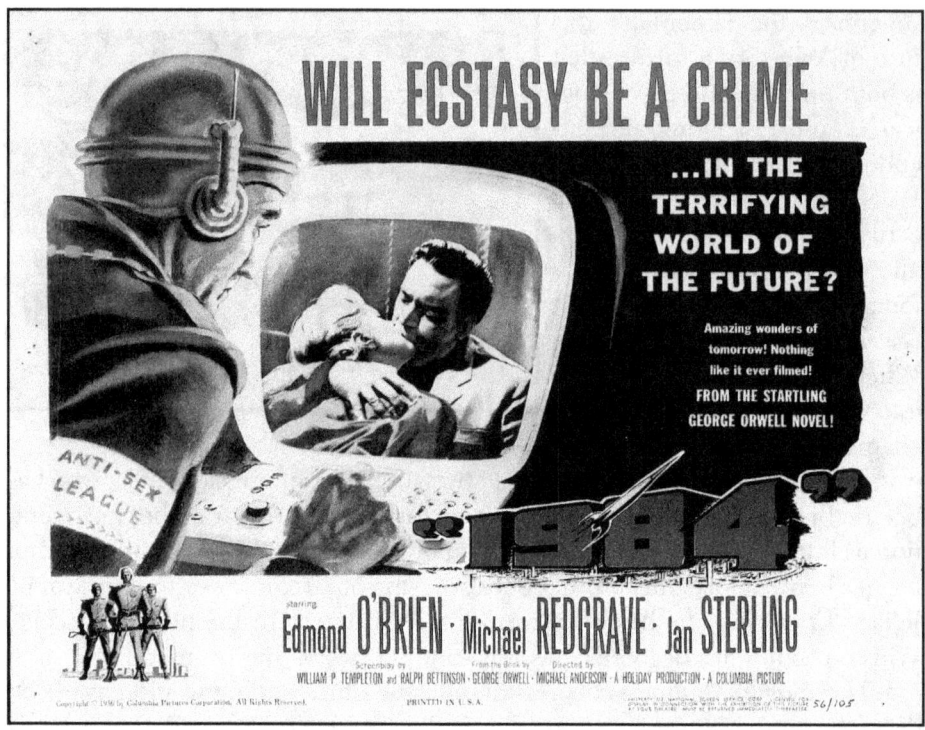

any other citizens who may be tempted to commit treason. They are aware of this but, because the torture has thoroughly extinguished their will to resist, they passively await the bullet that will crash into their brains. In the movie, there is no indication that they will be killed but they may as well be dead since the torture has drained all trace of humanity out of them.

As noted previously, this movie necessarily excludes many characters and events of the novel. For instance, the screenwriters omitted Winston's estranged wife, the result of a marriage that the Party ordered. Julia's membership in the Anti-Sex League and her wanton sexuality is also excluded, though other members of the League are briefly depicted. These omissions benefit the story since Winston's homicidal tendencies toward his wife and Julia's promiscuity would probably have decreased sympathy for the couple. Conversely, the movie includes the mirror scene from the novel but perhaps should have omitted it because, as filmed, it doesn't evoke the degree of sympathy for Winston that it should. In the novel, Winston's torturer forces him to look at himself in a three-way mirror after an extended period of suffering. Winston shockingly sees an emaciated, partially bald, partially toothless, grotesque remnant of a human being, looking like "a man of sixty suffering from some malignant disease." In the movie, Winston doesn't suffer such deformity and though he does look excessively shabby and debased, the shock effect is diminished.

Reference books often describe Michael Anderson as a competent but unexceptional director. This may be due to the fact that he worked within several genres and rarely displayed any kind of personal style. But while some of his work is admittedly routine, he also directed many exceptional movies. In 1955, he directed *The Dam Busters*, which the British Academy of Film and Television Arts (BAFTA) nominated for both a Best British Film of the Year Award and a Best Film from Any Source Award. *Shake Hands with the Devil* (1959), *The Wreck of the Mary Deare* (1959), *The Naked Edge* (1961), *Operation Crossbow* (1965) and *The Quiller Memorandum* (1966) are among his many movies that represent a variety of genres and display notable proficiency. As further testament to his talent, the Academy of Motion Picture Arts and Sciences (AMPAS) nominated him for a Best Director Academy Award for *Around the World in 80 Days* (1956) which was released just a few months after *1984*.

For *1984*, Anderson's style is largely unobtrusive in order to highlight the intelligent screenplay by Templeton and Bettinson. But when the scene demands it, he can be quite innovative. Several sequences offer indications of Anderson's eye for interesting compositions. For instance, when O'Connor begins to interrogate Smith, Anderson places his camera behind a seated Smith looking upward toward O'Connor's figure in the background; as the camera remains stationary, O'Connor walks toward the vulnerable prisoner, towers

Michael Redgrave instills his portrayal of O'Connor with an egotism that makes his sadism seem natural.

During an air raid, the Inner Party's Thought Police traverse the city to ensure that all Outer Party members take shelter.

over him, encircles him and then returns to the shadows, all the while speaking threateningly—and all in one seamless take. The director also stages the hate sessions very fluidly, creating a feeling of mounting excitement tinged with chilling hatred. Especially gripping is the scene in which Winston and Julia blissfully believe that they are enjoying intimacy and then suddenly realize that they are under surveillance. The Room 101 sequence is equally powerful. Instead of graphically depicting the rats, the director concentrates on Winston's terrified reaction to the escalating squealing of the rodents as they surge increasingly closer to his manacled face. This is a far more effective way of conveying the emotional intensity of the sequence and the reason for Winston's subsequent capitulation.

With the able assistance of C. Pennington Richards' cinematography and Terence Verity's art direction, Anderson impressively creates a nightmarish world of the future (totally the opposite of the garish future of his ostensibly utopian 1976 movie, *Logan's Run*). During the nighttime exterior scenes, everything within the landscape is dismal and filled with expressionistic shadows that reek of menace. The interiors are even shoddier. There is a claustrophobic feeling to Winston's confined room where the walls seem to envelop him. The Ministry of Truth relegates each of the workers to cramped cubicles, all subject to perpetual scrutiny. The Ministry of Love is devoid of any human warmth, complementing the instruments of torture contained within it. The pervasive dreariness of these settings contrasts with the sequences in which Winston and Julia enjoy their intimacy. Their genuine happiness obliterates the ruthless world that they believe they have evaded, which makes their ultimate fate so lamentable.

Though the movie is a British production, two Hollywood stars play the lead roles and it is probably not coincidental that they both have many film noirs among their credits. Edmond O'Brien's noirs include *D.O.A.* (1949), *711 Ocean Drive* (1950), *The Hitch-Hiker* (1953) and *Shield for Murder* (1954), which he also co-directed. Jan Sterling played roles in *Appointment with Danger* (1950), *Ace in the Hole* (1951), *Split Second* (1953) and *The Human Jungle* (1954), among others. Though they appeared in numerous other movies, in the mid-Fifties they were closely identified with the noir genre. Nevertheless, they perhaps received the most acclaim for playing different kinds of roles. The previous year, O'Brien had won a Best Supporting Actor Academy Award for his role as a sycophantic publicist in *The Barefoot Contessa*. That same year, Sterling had been nominated for a Best Supporting Actress Academy Award for her role as a former beauty queen in *The High and the Mighty*.

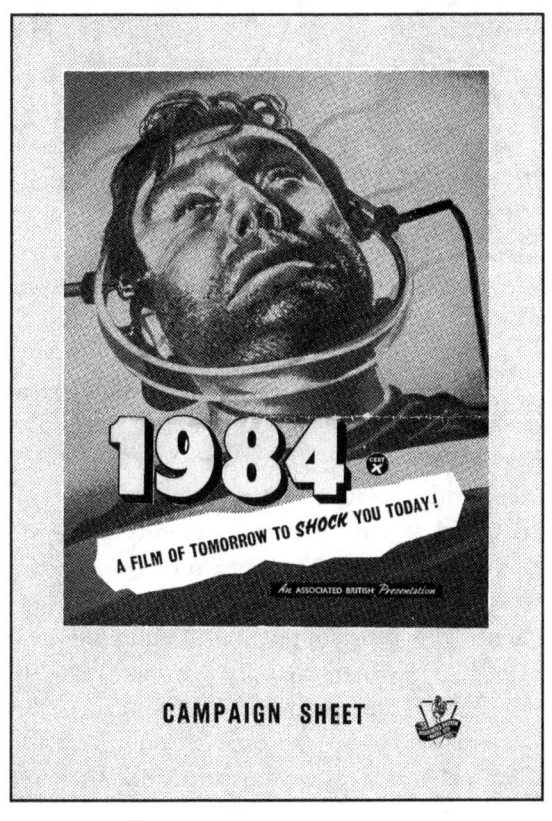

CAMPAIGN SHEET

The critics who claimed that O'Brien was miscast as Winston Smith because of his brawny physique as well as his age didn't understand that his portrayal is a "free adaptation" of Orwell's Smith. Though O'Brien is not the "smallish and frail figure" of the novel, his imposing physical presence actually makes his eventual collapse more shocking simply because he looks too robust to be reduced to such wretched submission. Regarding his age, O'Brien was thirty-nine when he filmed the movie, the same age as the novel's Smith. Regardless of the criticism, O'Brien is excellent. He initially instills his character with a sense of dignity as well as inner strength. He

Jan Sterling poses for a publicity photo.

is equally believable as a militant rebel and as a pitiful vassal. He is especially impressive in the extended torture sequence when he displays a variety of successive emotions, from defiance and anger to confusion and helplessness, until he totally breaks down and begs for mercy. As he sobbingly grovels into the arms of his tormentor, it is a truly pathetic sight and indicative of a superb performance.

In *Lost Films of the Fifties* (Citadel; 1988), Douglas Brode justly praises the actor's performance: "Edmond O'Brien neatly captured, in the entire film but especially in that last sequence, the dark vision that absolutely anyone can be broken on the modern rack of technology. The look in his eyes after having been completely stripped of his own ideas and emotions provides a terrifying warning of the power of the evolving police state. The role that O'Brien should be most remembered for is Winston Smith in *1984*."

Jan Sterling was a versatile performer and, although she frequently portrayed tough women in crime films, she could also play sympathetic characters. Because she doesn't have the "thick dark hair and freckled face" of Orwell's Julia, critics accused her of also being miscast. Furthermore, she was thirty-five years old, unlike the novel's twenty-seven-year-old Julia. But once again, this is the film's Julia who wants to be loved, not the novel's Julia who uses sex as a weapon. And being a similar age as O'Brien enables her to provide a credible chemistry for the couple that a younger actress would not have delivered. Moreover, she convincingly portrays a courageous woman possessing a longing not only to love and be loved but to simply enjoy fundamental human rights. The scene in which she puts on a dress for Winston is especially affecting because of the joy that she conveys at being able to display her femininity, a luxury denied to women by the Inner Party. The actress gives the distinct impression that her character has finally found an outlet for her suppressed love and her hope for happiness. At the finale, she poignantly makes Julia a pitiable character since it is clear that she has been purged of any trace of hope and happiness.

Michael Redgrave received a nomination for a Best Actor Academy Award for *Mourning Becomes Electra* (1947). He won the Best Actor Award at the Cannes

Film Festival for *The Browning Version* (1951). He was nominated twice for the BAFTA Best British Actor Award for *The Night My Number Came Up* (1955) and *Time Without Pity* (1957). *1984* was one of four movies he made with Michael Anderson, the others being *The Dam Busters*, *Shake Hands with the Devil* and *The Wreck of the Mary Deare*. As the treacherous O'Connor, his portrayal is extremely effective in part because it is restrained. He imbues O'Connor with a callous conceit that makes his brutality seem sickeningly natural. When he impatiently wipes his brow in the midst of inflicting pain upon his victim, the actor suggests that O'Connor sincerely believes in the righteousness of his merciless methods and that they are necessary to curing traitors of their sickness. It is a chilling portrait of a man who justifies his brutality as vital not only for the good of the state but for the good of his victims. Redgrave compellingly personifies this wretched inhumanity of the government that he represents.

Incidentally, O'Connor's counterpart in the novel is described as "a large burly man with a thick neck, brutal face and prizefighter's physique," which

Swedish poster for *1984*

does not at all fit Michael Redgrave. But detractors of Edmond O'Brien and Jan Sterling for not being similar to their counterparts in the novel were silent about Redgrave's similar variance. Possibly his history of being a Shakespearian actor on the stage gave him some slack with snobbish critics.

Despite *1984*'s current lack of status, it received many favorable reviews upon its release. The movie premiered in Great Britain in March 1956. *Variety*'s reviewer, Myro, was generally complimentary: "(This is) a grim depressing picture with a sinister glimpse of the future; Orwell's novel of the ultimate in totalitarian ruthlessness is faithfully presented." But from a box-office perspective, Myro wrote that the movie has "little entertainment value in the accepted sense of the word and will need special promotion." By the way, this review is of the version with the alternate ending which was released in the United Kingdom. Myro writes: "Winston and Julia's eventual murder by party guards brings the picture to an inconclusive end."

Several months later Columbia released *1984* in the United States, but this was the version with the indoctrination ending. Initially, it appears that the studio didn't know how to handle the movie. One of its earliest playdates was in Boston where it opened in July as the top feature of a double bill, the supporting movie being the British adventure film, *Storm Over the Nile*. In *The Boston Globe*, Marjorie Adams wrote: "The film has the same sense of bleak horror and black apprehension that Orwell developed when freedom was allowed to die; the conclusion is especially ironic and drearily logical as the lovers, aged and brainwashed so thoroughly that there is nothing left, can meet apathetically."

For subsequent bookings in major cities, the studio provided the movie with the type of special promotion that the bleak material required, booking it as a single feature into relatively small art house theaters. The movie had its New York City premiere in October at the Normandie Theater, an intimate

Italian poster for *1984*

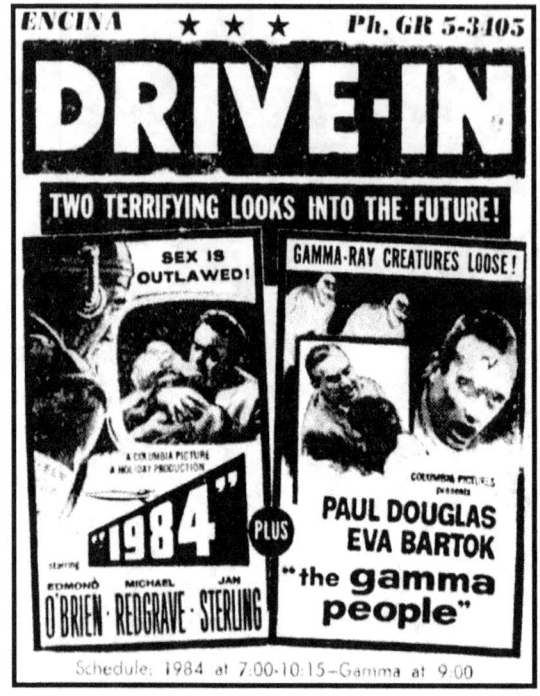

cinema known for presenting distinctive European and American films. In *The New York Times*, A. H. Weiler wrote: "*1984* is a stark, sober and thoughtful if not altogether persuasive film; the director and scenarists have retained the essential spirit and ideas of the novel and the lovers' vain attempt to capture moments of love is brought to a sardonic ending which gives this drama its basic power." *Newsweek*'s reviewer wrote: "What is most effectively upsetting is the prolonged view of brainwashing which occupies most of the movie's last moments; audiences will resent the unhappy ending while readers of the novel will resent the preoccupation with the love affair." *Time*'s reviewer wrote somewhat oddly: "Orwell's book was depressing partly because it was way too slick but the film is far more depressing as an anti-communist soap opera."

Based upon its playdates in major cities, the commercial prospects for *1984* appeared quite promising. In New York City, *Variety* reported that the movie earned "a great $10,200 in its first week, one of the top figures at the Normandie Theater." At the Plaza Theater in Washington D.C., it earned "a wow $11,000, virtually capacity for seven daily shows for this small-seater." If Columbia had continued to book the movie into specialty theaters, it would probably have achieved additional box-office success. Unfortunately, as *1984* made its way across the country, Columbia paired it with a low-budget science fiction quickie, *The Gamma People*, thereby making it appear to be a similar exploitation movie. For the double bill which played in conventional movie houses, the advertisement for *1984* depicted a helmet-wearing, sinister-looking soldier with an Anti-Sex League armband looking at a monitor that displays a couple kissing; the ominous question at the top of the poster titillated: "Will ecstasy be a crime in the terrifying world of the future?" Another tagline in an alternate poster promised even more salacious content: "Sex outlawed…in the terrifying world of tomorrow!" The equal-sized ad for the co-feature depicted a spooky figure under the tagline: "Gamma ghouls kill for their power-mad scientist ruler!" In view of this ill-advised marketing campaign, it is not surprising that adult audiences and admirers of the novel stayed away. On *Variety*'s list of top-grossing films of 1956, 116 movies earned more than the minimum of $1,000,000 in domestic theatrical rentals to qualify for inclusion. *1984* did not earn the minimum. Science fiction movies that earned positions on the list include *Forbidden Planet* (62nd with $1.6 million), *Invasion of the Body Snatchers* (89th with $1.2 million) and *Earth Vs. the Flying Saucers* (85th with $1.2 million).

The box-office failure of *1984* does not diminish its power. One message of this version of George Orwell's prophetic novel is that, in a totally tyrannical society, the desire for freedom will inevitably incite rebellion among subjugated people, even when the odds of succeeding are infinitesimal. Another message is that the oppressors will always utilize the infliction of excessive pain to crush insurgency. Most significantly, a totalitarian society will not only extinguish liberty but will annihilate any trace of individuality and completely destroy the human spirit. Michael Anderson's *1984* horrifyingly captures this message. In the closing sequence, Winston and Julia are both broken and transformed. Winston wants only to love Big Brother. Julia wants only to die. It is a frightening and unforgettable ending to a vastly underrated movie.

Credits: Producer: N. Peter Rathvon; Director: Michael Anderson; Screenplay: William P. Templeton, Ralph Bettinson, based upon the novel by George Orwell; Editor: Bill Lewthwaite; Cinematographer: C. Pennington Richards; Special Effects: George Blackwell, Bryan Langley, Norman Warwick; Music: Malcolm Arnold; Art Director: Terence Verity; Set Decoration: Olga Lehmann

Cast: Edmond O'Brien (Winston Smith); Michael Redgrave (O'Connor); Jan Sterling (Julia); David Kossoff (Charrington); Donald Pleasance (Parsons); Carol Wolveridge (Selina Parsons); Mervyn Johns (Jones); Ronan O'Casey (Rutherford); Patrick Allen (Ministry of Truth Official); Kenneth Griffiths (Prisoner); Michael Ripper (Outer Party Speaker); Ernest Clark (Outer Party Announcer); Ewen Solon (Outer Party Orator)

The Mind Benders

There is a terrifying moment in the 1963 movie, *The Mind Benders*, when the investigator, Major Hall and the researcher, Dr. Tate, realize that they cannot undo the damage that they have inflicted upon Dr. Henry Longman's brain. They have twisted and bent it into something unrecognizable and now they cannot untwist and unbend it. They have created a monster, but this monster has only one victim—his wife.

In *Science Fiction: The Film Encyclopedia* (William Morrow; 1984), Phil Hardy calls *The Mind Benders* "a fascinating, if flawed, film." It is a frightening movie because it presents its horror elements so casually and its practitioners so pretentious in their justification of their atrocious behavior. It is also a provocative movie that manages to survive an implausible ending.

To set the stage for the events that the movie will depict, a written statement follows the main credits: "This story was suggested by experiments on The Reduction of Sensation recently carried out at certain universities in the United States." In the 1950s, behavioral scientists conducted experiments on sensory deprivation, also known as perceptual isolation, using human beings as subjects. Sensory reduction means complete isolation of the subject from sight, sound, taste, touch and smell. The researchers hoped to determine the effects upon the human brain and the central nervous system when these senses are totally disconnected.

According to some accounts, the United States government funded the initial scientific experiments in sensory deprivation because of reports of suc-

cessful attempts by the Chinese Communists to brainwash American prisoners during the Korean War. The U.S. government also provided a more humanitarian purpose and stated that the scientists were attempting to determine how astronauts might survive extended periods in outer space while enduring isolation and zero gravity. Regardless of the motivation, the bizarre responses that the subjects frequently exhibited, as well as the damaging impact on their personalities, opened up new areas of research. This motivated the scientists to refocus onto the possibility of manipulating human behavior through alteration of the mind. Therein lies the basis for the horrifying experiments that followed and for the movie, *The Mind Benders*.

Scottish novelist James Kennaway, a pseudonym of James Ewing Peebles (1928-1968), had achieved fame for his first novel, *Tunes of Glory*, published in 1956; he also wrote the screenplay for the 1960 film version, for which he was nominated for both a BAFTA and an Academy Award. Kennaway had read accounts of the sensory reduction experiments and used them as the inspiration for an original screenplay that he wrote in the 1950s entitled *The Visiting Scientist* or *If This Be Treason*. However, since British film producers considered the subject matter to be too radical at the time, he went on to other projects. In 1958, he wrote a screenplay called *Violent Playground*  which producer Michael Relph and director Basil Dearden filmed, and which began the Relph-Dearden partnership. In the early 1960s, Relph and Dearden decided to film Kennaway's controversial script on sensory reduction, which the author re-titled *The Mind Benders*.

Filming of *The Mind Benders* occurred in the summer of 1962 at Pinewood Studios with some exteriors shot at Oxford University. While the movie was in production, Kennaway turned his screenplay into a novel which he published to coincide with the film's release. In 2014, Valancourt Books re-published the novel with a new introduction by Paul Gallagher who provided the above background information on the genesis of the screenplay. The novel quite naturally provides more detailed information on the scientific basis of the experiments as well as the actual experiments. Perhaps this is why John Clute in *The Science Fiction Encyclopedia* (Doubleday; 1970) calls the novel "borderline sf." In the same book, Brian Stableford writes: "Apredominant issue is the prospect of mind control, or brainwashing, which plays a key part in George Orwell's *1984* and which has become a standard element in dystopian fiction; stories focusing on the possibilities in this area include (among others) *The Mind Benders* by James

Major Hall (John Clements), Dr. Tate (Michael Bryant) and Oonagh Longman (Mary Ure) locate Dr. Henry Longman (Dirk Bogarde) and Annabella (Wendy Craig) in the laboratory near the isolation tank.

Kennaway." However, unlike Winston Smith, the protagonist of this story actually volunteers for his torture.

The movie begins with the shocking suicide of Oxford University Professor Dr. Sharpey, a research scientist who had been working for the British government by participating in tests involving sensory reduction and isolation. After police find a suitcase filled with money next to Sharpey's body, Army Investigator Major Hall deduces that the professor who had leftist sympathies had become a double agent who was also working for the Communists. This first part of the movie tends to be slow and deliberate as the script establishes the foundation for the story with an explanatory description of the scientific basis for the ensuing experiments. This explanation is accompanied by research films showing subjects of sensory deprivation and their appalling psychological after-effects.

Dr. Daniel Tate, Sharpey's laboratory assistant, informs Major Hall that Dr. Henry Longman, who had also been working with Sharpey, has taken an extended leave of absence from the university. Hall requires the assistance of Longman to find out the truth about the experiments and tracks him down at his home. Longman is loyal to Sharpey and is certain that he could not have committed treason. Furthermore, he believes that the experiments may have made him vulnerable to brainwashing and hypnotic suggestion which caused his mental deterioration and suicide. In view of Longman's insistence on Sharpey's innocence, Hall persuades him to undergo similar testing to disprove Sharpey's guilt. Longman is so self-assured that he believes that he can withstand the dangerous consequences of the experiments and that he can prevent his mind from manipulation. This will prove to be Longman's disastrous mistake.

The story then unfolds in an increasingly horrifying manner that begins the moment that Longman enters the isolation tank. Actually, this may be the film's basic flaw. Before he essentially agrees to be a guinea pig, Longman is already frightened of the effects of further experiments upon his own sanity. In fact, it was because he was so distraught over the tests that he left the university to find solace with his loving wife, Oonagh. In view of this, it strains credibility that he will so willingly participate in similar tests and thus disregard his wife and their four children. Then again, he basks in his self-assurance and in his belief that he can outsmart this supercilious government agent. So, the flaw may not be in the screenplay but in Longman's personality which sets the groundwork for his deterioration.

Longman is placed in the isolation tank with a wetsuit and breathing apparatus for eight hours. With Tate's assistance, Hall is determined to find out if extended immersion in the tank can change a subject's personality as well as

Tate (Michael Bryant) and his assistant Norman (Terry Palmer) help Longman (Dirk Bogarde) out of his wetsuit following his first immersion into the isolation tank.

his emotions. When Longman emerges from the tank, he appears to have suffered a complete mental collapse. Hall realizes that, due to his fragile and vulnerable condition, Longman is now susceptible to indoctrination, or brainwashing, and may be able to provide an explanation for Sharpey's breakdown. To prove this theory, Hall speculates that he has to destroy one of Longman's basic beliefs, specifically his love for his wife. Tate at first objects but then agrees for reasons that will later become obvious. They then meticulously implant in Longman's mind the false beliefs that Oonagh has been unfaithful to him and that he has never loved her.

Later, after Longman appears to recover from his ordeal, he insists that the test had no effect upon him. Though he seems to be in control of his emotions, it will later become apparent that the sensory deprivation has reduced him to a pliable empty shell of a man whose mind has become susceptible to total manipulation by his handlers. However, since he appears to be his usual self, Hall and Tate accept the apparent failure of their experiment. Seemingly unharmed, Longman returns home to his wife. This is only the beginning of the long nightmare of living hell for Oonagh Longman.

Major Hall and Dr. Tate are in some ways modern and more sophisticated versions of Baron Victor Frankenstein from Hammer's production of *The Curse*

Tate implants within Longman's brain the belief that his wife has been unfaithful and that he never loved her.

of Frankenstein five years earlier. Indeed, at one point, Tate says to Hall: "This is strictly Frankenstein company, only this time it's fact." While the Baron inserted the damaged brain of a professor into his creature's body, Hall and Tate instead work with the subject's existent brain and turn, twist and bend it into something totally different, thus making the subject a distorted version of his former self. In the same detached style displayed by Baron Frankenstein, Hall and Tate invade Longman's mind to determine if they can alter his fundamental beliefs. Consequently, the person that Henry Longman becomes may not be physically repellent like Frankenstein's creature but he is just as much a monster, perhaps even more so since he becomes a sadistic human being who psychologically tortures his wife. Longman's hubris as much as the cavalier insensitivity of his tormentors has damaged his life and his family, perhaps irreparably.

It is not until several months later that Hall and Tate discover that their mind-altering strategy has worked extremely well with disastrous consequences. Hall begins to learn the truth accidentally when he attends a party for university employees. Hall is surprised to see Longman frolicking with a single woman, Annabella. This persuades Hall to bring Tate to Longman's home where they become aware of the horror that Longman has been inflicting upon his wife. At Hall's urging, Oonagh tells them about her vacation with her

Longman sarcastically resists attempts by Hall and Tate to undo the damage they have done to his brain while Annabella seems confused.

Science Fiction Thrills...Horror Chills

Longman begins to feel remorse as Oonagh (Mary Ure) experiences labor pains.

husband and his repeated shaming of her throughout Europe but especially in Amsterdam. Hall is shocked at the consequences of the experiment while Tate confesses reluctantly to his ambivalent reasons for not maintaining close observation of Longman. Hall becomes determined to reverse the results of the experiment and hopes that playing the tapes of the indoctrination will reverse the damage. Unfortunately, their expert brainwashing worked so well that Longman now accepts as truth the false assertions about Oonagh.

Shortly thereafter, the happy resolution suddenly occurs. During a hostile altercation, Longman pushes Oonagh away from him and she suddenly begins to experience labor pains. Longman appears to feel some degree of remorse and subsequently assists his wife in giving birth to their fifth child. Upon the joy of becoming a father again, he returns to his former self. This ending is frankly not convincing and ends the film on a romantic note that doesn't fit in with all that has preceded it. Indeed, when Annabella becomes sentimental at the sight of the newborn baby, the movie enters a stream of mawkishness that threatens to derail it.

Director Basil Dearden filmed *The Mind Benders* in the realistic black-and-white style that many British domestic dramas and thrillers utilized during this period. And this movie is as much a domestic drama as a thriller. The espionage angle more or less recedes into the background as the story progresses. The science fictional elements are also minimized as the marital drama takes precedence. The director's emphasis on realism results in an almost documentary-style effect for the film's beginning. But Dearden initiates the tension when Longman is placed in the isolation tank. Assisted greatly by cinematographer Denys Coop, there is a haunting image of Longman floating in water, resembling Frankenstein's monster on the Baron's elevated operating table.

The suspense accelerates when Hall and Tate release Longman from the tank. Dearden deludes audiences the same way that Longman deludes himself as well as Hall and Tate. Longman seems perfectly fine as he leaves the laboratory. The first indication of Longman's transformation occurs when Oonagh drives him home and stops at a secluded place, the scene of a previous rendezvous, to tell him that she is pregnant. Up until this time, Longman appears to be his former self, totally in love with his wife and with no apparent change in his personality. But then Dearden closes in on Longman's face and darkens the area around his eyes. The sheer hatred in his eyes presages the horror that will follow.

Dirk Bogarde gives a splendid performance as Dr. Henry Longman. He projects genuine warmth as the affectionate husband and loving father. And yet with equal conviction he conveys sheer pleasure as the coldhearted tormentor. Perhaps Bogarde's best scene in the movie is when Longman collapses in tears into Tate's arms and begs not to be put back into the tank. He is so convincing that it is almost embarrassing to see his character reduced to such

Longman is considering Tate's request to participate in the sensory reduction tests which Oonagh (Mary Ure) vehemently opposes.

a state. Mary Ure evokes sympathy as Oonagh with her quiet acceptance of her husband's cruelty; her key expressions reveal that she accepts her condition not out of masochism but for the sake of her children as well as her unborn child. John Clements conveys both sides of Major Hall, from the detached investigator to the conscience-stricken rescuer. Michael Bryant has a difficult role because Tate must conceal his conflicted motivations for his behavior due to his feelings for Oonagh, but he successfully creates a character who is struggling with his emotions.

Throughout their 12-year partnership, producer Michael Relph and director Basil Dearden made many popular entertainments, such as *The League of Gentlemen* (1960) and *The Assassination Bureau* (1969). However, they were perhaps best known for their films that tackled sensitive issues. In addition to *Violent Playground* (1958) which concerned juvenile delinquency, their movies include *Sapphire* (1959) about racial prejudice, *Victim* (1961) about homosexuality and *Walk in the Shadow* aka *Life for Ruth* (1962), about religious convictions. They didn't shy away from controversial topics and brought the same type of analytical criticism to *The Mind Benders*.

The Mind Benders failed at the box-office on both sides of the Atlantic. This was somewhat surprising in the United Kingdom in view of Dirk Bogarde's popularity. It is possible that the subject matter turned people off. Also, Dr. Henry Longman was a far cry from Dr. Simon Sparrow in the series of very popular comedies that Bogarde made in the 1950s. (Bogarde returned to the role for the last time in *Doctor in Distress* which was released five months after *The Mind Benders* and was far more popular.) In the United States, American-International gave the movie an exclusive opening at two specialty houses in New York City but a negative review in *The New York Times* ("This Relph-Dearden experiment doesn't hold water.") and poor box office doomed its future commercial prospects. American-International, known at this time for its beach party movies, subsequently released it in many parts of the country as a supporting feature to a World War II B movie called *Operation Bikini*. Audiences stayed away in droves. Consequently, *The Mind Benders* didn't earn the minimum

of $1,000,000 in domestic theatrical rentals to qualify for a position on *Variety*'s list of top-grossing films of 1963. This must have been discouraging for Relph and Dearden, especially since something called *Hootenanny Hoot* and the Japanese *King Kong Vs. Godzilla* earned enough to be listed. The good news is that *Operation Bikini* didn't make the list either.

Despite the optimistic ending of *The Mind Benders*, the horrific realism of the hazards that scientific experimentation can inflict upon average people remains the film's foremost message. The fact that experiments similar to those that the film depicts occurred—and probably still occur—in prestigious universities and in government laboratories adds to the shock of the message. This is an exceptionally disturbing movie because it depicts scientists and military leaders committing inhumane acts for the advancement of scientific knowledge and in the name of national security. This happened more than half a century ago. Who knows what such people are capable of today?

Credits: Producer: Michael Relph; Director: Basil Dearden; Screenplay: James Kennaway; Cinematographer: Denys Coop; Editor: John D. Guthridge; Music: Georges Auric; Art Director: Jim Morahan

Cast: Dirk Bogarde (Dr. Henry Longman); Mary Ure (Oonagh Longman); John Clements (Major Hall); Michael Bryant (Dr. Tate); Wendy Craig (Annabella); Harold Goldblatt (Professor Sharpey); Geoffrey Keen (Calder); Terry Palmer (Norman); Norman Bird (Aubrey); Teresa Van Hoorn (Penny Longman); Georgina Moon (Persephone Longman); Timothy Beaton (Paul Longman); Christopher Ellis (Peers Longman)

Crack in the World

An ancient philosopher once said: "Be kind to the earth and do not harm it because it is far more powerful than you are."

Dr. Stephen Sorensen of Project Inner Space should have heeded these words of advice. Despite the fact that his motives are beneficial, he unleashes the full force of nature which threatens to destroy the entire planet. This is the plot of the movie, *Crack in the World*, which Paramount released in 1965. It could be called a disaster movie, though it was not until the following decade that the term became popular. Today some of the film's disparagers sneer at its erroneous science but this movie preceded the formulation of the Plate Tectonics Theory. Since that knowledge was not yet officially acknowledged in 1965, the movie establishes its own logical rules based upon knowledge at that time and then intelligently proceeds from that base.

Andrew Marton, the director of *Crack in the World*, may today be best known as a Second Unit Director, particularly for his work on action scenes in such movies as *Ben-Hur* (1959) and *Cleopatra* (1963). But he had been directing since 1928 and his resumé included co-directing *King Solomon's Mines* (1950) and the American exterior sequences for *The Longest Day* (1962). Another highlight of Marton's career is *The Wild North* (1952), an adventure movie that depicted, though in a totally different manner, the dangers inherent within the natural world. *Crack in the World* contains plausible plot twists while the suspense develops at an increasingly menacing pace. Marton maintains an escalating momentum as scenes of devastation bring the impending apocalypse increasingly closer. He also manages to interject the romantic complications without impairing the primary narrative. As a result, the movie contains no unnecessary padding, thanks also to the extremely well-constructed script.

Ted Rampion (Kieron Moore), Maggie Sorenson (Janette Scott), Markov (Gary Lasdun) and Rand (Jim Gillen) frantically try to stop a train speeding toward a collapsing bridge.

Jon Manchip White and Julian Halevy wrote the screenplay based upon White's original story. This is one of only two screenplays from White who wrote primarily for British television; he was more prolific as an author of numerous novels as well as works of non-fiction. Halevy, a pseudonym for Julian Zimet, started his Hollywood career in 1941, writing mostly B westerns; he was blacklisted in the 1950s but resumed his career the following decade. Executive Producer Philip Yordan, who had a history of "fronting" for blacklisted writers, reportedly hired Halevy to re-write White's screenplay and the two writers apparently didn't work together. Regardless, the resultant script is an enthralling story that is rich in character detail while it progresses from one catastrophic disaster to another, each one building closer to an ending which promises to be, quite literally, earth-shattering.

Crack in the World begins in Africa, where a team of international scientists has established the Project Inner Space laboratory two miles beneath the earth's surface. Dr. Sorensen and his team of idealistic geophysicists have tunneled into the earth in hopes of obtaining an infinite supply of energy from the magma at the earth's core. But a final impenetrable shell shields the earth's center and prevents the team from reaching the magma. Sorensen wants to detonate a thermonuclear warhead to penetrate this final crust. However, due to existing fissures caused by previous underground atomic testing, geologist Ted Rampion believes that exploding a nuclear missile through the center of the earth could create disastrous geologic ramifications.

Ted and Maggie attempt to persuade Dr. Stephen Sorenson (Dana Andrews) to leave the laboratory with them.

Sorensen also has personal problems, as apparent from the strain between him and Maggie, his younger wife. Maggie wants to start a family and is hurt by her husband's refusal. Furthermore, Maggie previously was romantically involved with Rampion. Neither Maggie nor Rampion know that Sorensen is receiving radiation treatment for cancer which is one reason why he so urgently wants to complete his mission before anyone else can assume control of the project. He also knows that further delays will result in a termination of the project. On a more altruistic level, he is insistent on acting immediately because he genuinely wants to benefit the human race. However, perhaps unconsciously, he may have another motive; due to personal and professional pride, he has to justify himself to Maggie and show her that he is more knowledgeable than Rampion.

Sorensen persists and is able to persuade the project's director and grant supervisor, Dr. Charles Eggerston and his commission, of the viability of his proposal. Rampion races to London to try to persuade Eggerston of the potential dangers but he presents his argument too late. At the same time, Sorensen's doctor informs him that his cancer is incurable. To ensure his legacy, he detonates the powerful nuclear bomb which succeeds in cracking the crust surrounding the magma. Initially, as molten magma erupts to the surface, it appears that the blast has been successful. However, it soon becomes apparent that the explosion has created a new fissure that is rapidly expanding and affecting every area of the globe. The resulting volcanic eruptions, earthquakes and tidal waves kill thousands of people in one day. More alarmingly, if the fissure continues to expand, it threatens to divide the entire planet. The scientists begin a race against time to save the earth and the human race. Rampion deduces that detonating another atomic bomb inside a volcano could seal the crack and stop the fissure's expansion. But instead of stopping the pressure, the second bomb causes the crack to reverse its course to create a massive ring that will ignite at the laboratory. This could be nature's display of dispensing poetic justice as the scientists will now have to rapidly evacuate the laboratory.

On a personal note, the fact that events prove Sorensen's theory to be erroneous destroys his self-confidence. He now has to face imminent death with the knowledge that he has failed professionally and personally. He takes out his anger upon Maggie who can't understand his unkindness. Of course, these personal problems recede into the distance once the destruction of the planet and the end of human life become practically a certainty. It is a credit to the film that this undercurrent of personal problems assumes relative insignificance but still has an impact upon the development of events and, specifically, upon Sorensen's climactic act of expiation.

The production of *Crack in the World* originated with frozen funds. After a controversial Hollywood career, Philip Yordan settled in Spain and wrote several large-scale spectacles for producer Samuel Bronston, including *El Cid*, *King of Kings* and *55 Days at Peking*. According to his account, he produced *Crack in the World* under his own Security Pictures banner along with another

Sorenson oversees the central operations at the Project Inner Space laboratory.

science fiction film, *The Day of the Triffids* (1963), "to free up my frozen pesetas." In 1964, he negotiated a deal for Paramount Pictures to distribute *Crack in the World*. Filming took place in Spain on location and at CEA Studios and Samuel Bronston Studios in Madrid from the end of April to mid-July 1964, followed by two weeks additional shooting in the Canary Islands.

An article in the May 2 1964 issue of *Variety* states: "The $100,000 Central Operations facility was the biggest set ever built at CEA Studios up to that time." So while this was not an expensive movie by Bronson standards, it was not cheap either. Indeed, the movie includes very impressive special effects which are quite remarkable considering its relatively moderate budget. Eugene Lourie supervised the special effects while Alex Weldon greatly assisted with the on-site handiwork. Lourie was the director of such monster movies as *The Beast from 20,000 Fathoms* and *Gorgo* while Alex Weldon had created some of the effects for Bronson's spectacles. Their effects are nothing short of spectacular. It is difficult to believe that the scenes of natural disasters are actually scale models, the reality of which is greatly assisted by some superb matte paintings. Though uncredited, Francisco Prosper created the miniatures while Charles-Henri Assola constructed the models with Basilio Cortijo contributing to the effectiveness of the cataclysmic scenes. Manuel Berenguer's terrific technicolor cinematography is another asset. Also worthy of mention is the score by John Douglas which includes a doom-laden main theme that complements the inevitability of the worldwide catastrophe.

Ted and John Masefield (Peter Damon) descend into the volcanic crater to drop the second atomic bomb.

Crack in the World contains many memorable sequences. The deep-sea submarine that locates the flaming fissure at the bottom of the ocean is believably realistic. Equally noteworthy is the scene depicting the scientists descending into the volcanic crater and trying to situate the second atomic bomb before the extreme heat dissolves their heat-resistant suits. Also unforgettable are the scenes depicting the interior of the volcano and a speeding train atop a collapsing bridge. Scenes of destruction and panic lead to the exhilarating climactic sequence depicting the convergence of the fissures and the hurling of a portion of the earth into the atmosphere. The last scene in which Maggie and Rampion gaze in awe at the new moon is both distressing and inspiring. This denouement elicits solemn reflection of the dangers of tampering with the earth.

The movie's message is understated which makes it more stimulating. The film speaks against the use of atomic and nuclear devices but in an unobtrusive manner. Most of all perhaps, the movie illustrates the ar-

Ted and Maggie witness the birth f a new moon.

Science Fiction Thrills...Horror Chills

rogance of mere mortals who audaciously believe that they can control nature. When the destruction of the planet seems imminent, Eggerston asks Rampion: "Is there anything we can do?" Ted's answer is simple: "Pray." This brief exchange of dialogue reminds the scientists of their need for humility, though it is a lesson learned at a tremendous cost. Indeed, the ease with which nature destroys the multi-million-dollar Project Inner Space is a shocking reminder that no amount of money or ingenuity can justify the laboratory's intrusion into the sanctity of the planet. Incidentally, at the beginning of the movie, there is a brief but telling shot of primitive African natives with spears and shields gazing down upon the representatives of advanced civilization speeding toward the laboratory and, at this point, unknowingly hastening the world's destruction. This fleeting shot emphasizes the message that scientists have to realize that advanced technology and superior knowledge requires a moral responsibility toward the entire human race.

Dana Andrews had been a major star in the 1940s and early 1950s but by the mid-1960s he was playing supporting roles in A movies while starring in B movies. But he never stopped giving A-level performances and his portrayal of Dr. Stephen Sorensen is splendid. His sober, understated acting style gives the film a crucial authority that helps immensely in bringing credibility to the proceedings. At key moments in the film, his expressions reveal his total im-

Italian lobby card features Janette Scott and Kieron Moore.

Sorenson's bandaged hand reveals his radiation treatment of which Ted and Maggie are now aware.

mersion into his role. For instance, his lack of response when Maggie attempts to make love to him is as informative as his satisfaction when he believes that his plan has succeeded. And then there is that moment when the actor must convey Sorensen's humiliation by publicly admitting that his strategy has tragically failed. Andrews provides an earnest and sympathetic performance that is multilayered because he suggests that Sorensen may be acting not only to selflessly help the human race but also out of hubris. Because of Sorensen's personal problems, Andrews conveys the possibility that his character may be putting pride over world security. Andrews creates an intelligent but fallible character whose utmost desire is to benefit the world but whose personal problems may have affected his judgement.

Janette Scott as Maggie and Kieron Moore as Rampion complement Andrews' performance with credible portrayals. It is illustrative of their performances that they infuse their characters with the emotion that Sorensen deliberately suppresses. Their sincerity ensures that the human drama never approaches a soap opera level, though it adds a layer of tension to many scenes. Both of their characters are not stereotypical, thanks to the shadings they bring to their roles. Scott's Maggie is also a scientist and her expressions at times indicate that, while she totally supports her husband, she may have some

misgivings about his theory. In a key scene, Moore's Rampion doesn't hesitate to attack Sorensen's vanity and, after events prove his theory to have been the correct one, he displays no satisfaction. Alexander Knox's portrayal of Eggerston is little more than a cameo but he also impresses with his usual convincing performance.

Many reference books express admiration for *Crack in the World*. In *A Pictorial History of Science Fiction Films* (Citadel Press; 1976), Jeff Rovin writes: "The film is lavishly mounted and well-acted, and it makes for solid entertainment." In *The Great Science Fiction Pictures* (Scarecrow; 1977), James Robert Parish and Michael R. Pitts write: "The movie benefits greatly from Dana Andrews' well-modulated performance as the slightly unethical scientist who almost destroys the world." However, in *The Science Fiction Encyclopedia* (Doubleday; 1979), John Brosnan writes: "This ambitious idea is undermined by a weak script and too small a budget."

Paramount promoted *Crack in the World* as an exploitation movie that studio executives perhaps hoped would quickly recoup its investment. To hasten this objective, the sensational advertisements for the movie proclaimed in large letters: "Thank God It's Only a Motion Picture!" It premiered in Los Angeles citywide in February 1965 but didn't appear in the New York City area

Ted and Maggie struggle to climb the damaged elevator shaft to escape the destruction of the laboratory.

until May when it opened in neighborhood theaters on a double bill with a British movie, *A Boy Ten Feet Tall*. Howard Thompson in *The New York Times* called it "trim, engrossing, beautifully written (and) the best science fiction thriller this year." Yet it attracted meagre audiences. On *Variety*'s annual list of top-grossing films of 1965, it didn't earn the minimum domestic theatrical rentals of one million dollars to qualify for inclusion on the list. It is also informative that not a single science fiction movie is on the list.

Crack in the World is an underrated science fiction thriller that is exciting and challenging. It is a poignant human drama as well as a spectacular adventure. And it is a reminder to scientists that they should always listen to those ancient philosophers.

German poster for *Crack in the World*

Credits: Executive Producer: Philip Yordan; Producers: Bernard Glasser, Lester A. Sansom; Director: Andrew Marton; Screenplay: Jon Manchip White, Julian Halevy, based upon a story by John Manchip White; Cinematographer: Manuel Berenguer; Editor: Derek Parsons; Music: John Douglas; Special Effects Director and Art Director: Eugene Lourie; Special Effects: Alex Weldon; Costumes: Laure de Zarate

Cast: Dana Andrews (Dr. Stephen Sorensen); Janette Scott (Dr. Maggie Sorensen); Kieron Moore (Dr. Ted Rampion); Alexander Knox (Sir Charles Eggerston); Peter Damon (John Masefield); Jim Gillen (Rand); Gary Lasdun (Markov); Alfred Brown (Dr. Bill Evans); Mike Steen (Steele); Sydna Scott (Angela); John Karlsen (Dr. Reynolds); Todd Martin (Simpson); Ben Tatar (Indian Ambassador)

The Mummy's Shroud

Back in the 1960s, theaters still presented double features which included the main feature and a supporting feature. The movie that topped the bill was an A movie while a B movie occupied the bottom of the bill. B movies were usually inexpensive and often had relatively low production qualities as well as second-tier personnel in front of and behind the camera. Audiences bought tickets to see the main feature and didn't expect much of the supporting movie. On some occasions, however, the movie at the bottom of the bill proved to be at least moderately entertaining. England's Hammer Films had a reputation for infusing their supporting features with some degree of professionalism. They weren't great movies, but they weren't bad movies either. They were B movies and shouldn't be judged by the standards of A movies. By such standards, *The Mummy's Shroud* is better than average.

By 1967, the glory days of Hammer Films were on the wane. Hammer's ascendancy began ten years earlier with the release of *The Curse of Frankenstein* (1957) and entered its peak years with *Horror of Dracula* (1958), both of which were directed by Terence Fisher and starred Peter Cushing and Christopher Lee. Among the many excellent films that Hammer produced during its most creative period was *The Mummy* (1959), another Fisher-Cushing-Lee collabora-

tion. However, unlike the Dracula and Frankenstein movies, Hammer didn't make a sequel to their mummy film, despite its success. Hammer did eventually return to mummy territory, though it was not a sequel. *The Curse of the Mummy's Tomb* (1964) played the lower-half of a double bill with Hammer's *The Gorgon* (ironically still another Fisher-Cushing-Lee movie) and was quickly forgotten, being decidedly inferior to its predecessor.

After this disappointment, Hammer waited three years to make another mummy movie. The title was *The Mummy's Shroud* (1967) and it attracted even less

The mummy (Eddie Powell) strangles Claire (Maggie Kimberly); this scene is not in the movie and is a publicity photo.

attention than the second movie. Hammer released it as a supporting feature to the studio's *Frankenstein Created Woman* (Fisher-Cushing sans Lee) and those critics who bothered to see it gave it scathing reviews. Contemporary reference books give it little if any respect. In the book, *Hammer, the House of Horror* (Overlook Press; 1996), Howard Maxford calls it "a less than routine affair." In *The Encyclopedia of the Horror Movies* (Harper & Row; 1986), Phil Hardy writes:

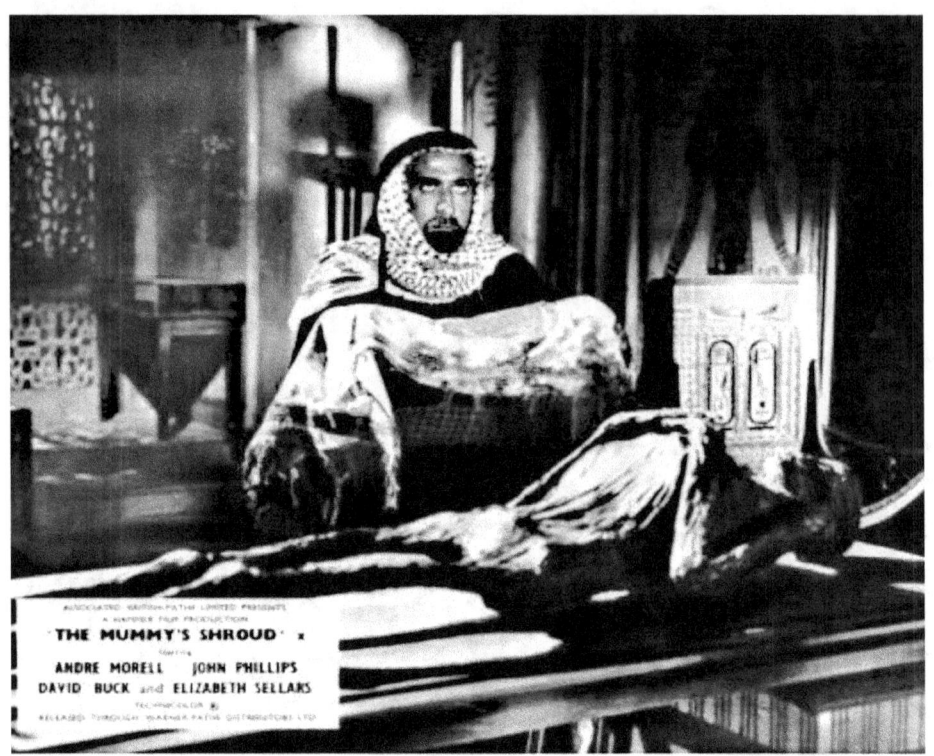

Hasmid (Roger Delgado) angrily intends to use the shroud to revive Prem.

"Hammer's third entry in its mummy series continues the downward slide from (the first) movie." In his annual *Movie Guide* (Signet; multiple editions), Leonard Maltin gives it his lowest rating and calls it a "bomb." Even the director of the movie, John Gilling, expressed disdain for it; in Wayne Kinsey's book, *Hammer, the Bray Studio Years* (Reynolds & Hearn; 2002), Gilling states that he wasn't proud of the movie and considered it one of his worst. Only Marcus Hearn and Alan Barnes in *The Hammer Story* (Titan Books; 1997) give it mild praise, calling it "an accomplished second feature."

The Mummy's Shroud admittedly is inferior to the 1959 movie. Its economical budget is obvious and the plot is a retread of previous movies in which a mummy is brought back to life to wreak vengeance upon the blasphemers who desecrated its tomb. Also, this mummy's make-up seems somewhat bland. However, to counter these deficiencies, it has some assets, among them Hammer's typically fine attention to period detail, some clever departures from the familiar plot, well-developed characterizations and fine ensemble acting.

The Mummy's Shroud begins in 2000 BC in ancient Egypt. Palace intrigues drive the Pharaoh's young son, Kah-to-Bey, and his loyal slave, Prem, into the desert. When the boy dies, Prem places a sacred shroud over his body and buries him. In 1920, an archaeological expedition financed by wealthy industrialist Stanley Preston searches for Kah-to-Bey's crypt. Sir Basil Walden leads the expedition which includes Preston's son, Paul, along with linguist Claire de Sangre and photographer Harry Newton. After the expedition is reported missing, Preston and his wife Barbara arrive in Cairo. Preston organizes a search party, which he reluctantly joins, to find the expedition and orders his lackey, Longbarrow, to accompany him. Meanwhile, Sir Basil and his party discover Kah-to-Bey's grave just before Preston and his party find them.

Sir Basil (Andre Morell) uncovers the shroud of Kah-to-Bey.

They ignore the threats of Hasmid, the keeper of the tomb, who warns of death to anyone who desecrates the grave. When a snake bites Sir Basil, this seems to be the first indication that they should heed Hasmid's warning. Nevertheless, they unearth the mummified bodies of the shrouded Kah-to-Bey and Prem. Though Claire anxiously refuses to decipher the words on the shroud, they take their discovery back to Cairo. Preston secretly has Basil committed to an asylum and assumes full credit for the expedition's success. But Hasmid, aided by his fortune-telling mother, steals the shroud and reads the words of death which bring Prem back to life. One by one, the mummy exacts his vengeance against four desecrators until the last two survivors desperately try to stop the curse.

Dickie Owen plays Prem, Kah-to-Bey's loyal servant.

This summary of the plot has a ring of familiarity for anyone who has seen previous mummy films, including Universal's movies from the 1940s. The lengthy prologue elicited some criticism for its exposition, but it is necessary to fully understand the tragedy of the ill-fated boy and his loyal slave. Evil triumphs in ancient Egypt; the benevolent pharaoh is murdered and his son, the rightful heir to the throne, dies soon afterward. Prem's devotion to his young master assumes a tragic component because he was unable to protect the boy and restore him to his

Science Fiction Thrills...Horror Chills

Museum curator (Andre Malandrinos) studies the remains of Kah-to-Bey.

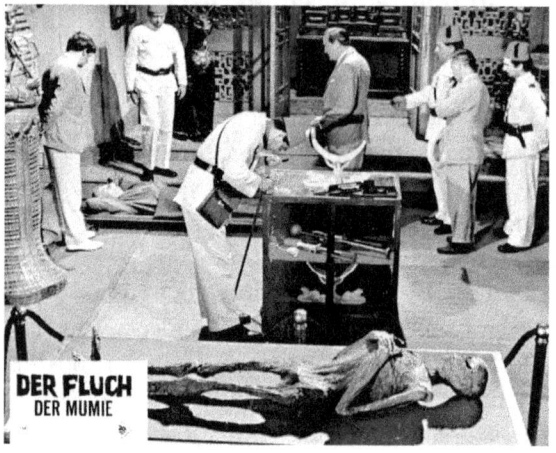

Police officials study Sir Basil's body.

throne. Thus, his desire for vengeance after death is totally unselfish. In view of this, it is possible to view Prem as the film's only noble character. The members of Sir Basil's crew possess the conceit of many Europeans of the era whose assumption of moral superiority routinely disregarded the culture of people whom they consider inferior to them. For this transgression, they will be punished. There is perhaps some fairness to the fact that only those who beg forgiveness of Prem will be spared a horrible death.

The film contains detailed characterizations. Stanley Preston is an arrogant, pompous braggart who has concern only for himself. He is accustomed to getting his way, usually by means of bribery or force. As his fear mounts, he will even abandon his wife and son to escape death. Barbara Preston never expresses any feelings for her husband but her expressions at key moments signify her contempt for him. Indeed, the pleasure with which she enjoys his fear and impending death is chilling. Paul Preston also displays some unexpected backbone when he turns against his father. Sir Basil appears to be a kindhearted person whose consideration for his colleagues takes precedence over his own ambitions. Among his colleagues, there is no hint of romance, which is a welcome twist. Claire is just another member of the expedition whose linguistic skill is needed. Claire is also somewhat different from the usual heroine in that she instinctively senses from the beginning that there may be more than superstition to the sacred shroud. It is this respect for other cultures that will save her and Paul from a grisly fate. This same respect will allow her to restore the shroud to Kah-to-Bey, which signifies the culpability of the expedition. Inspector Barrani, the local police officer in

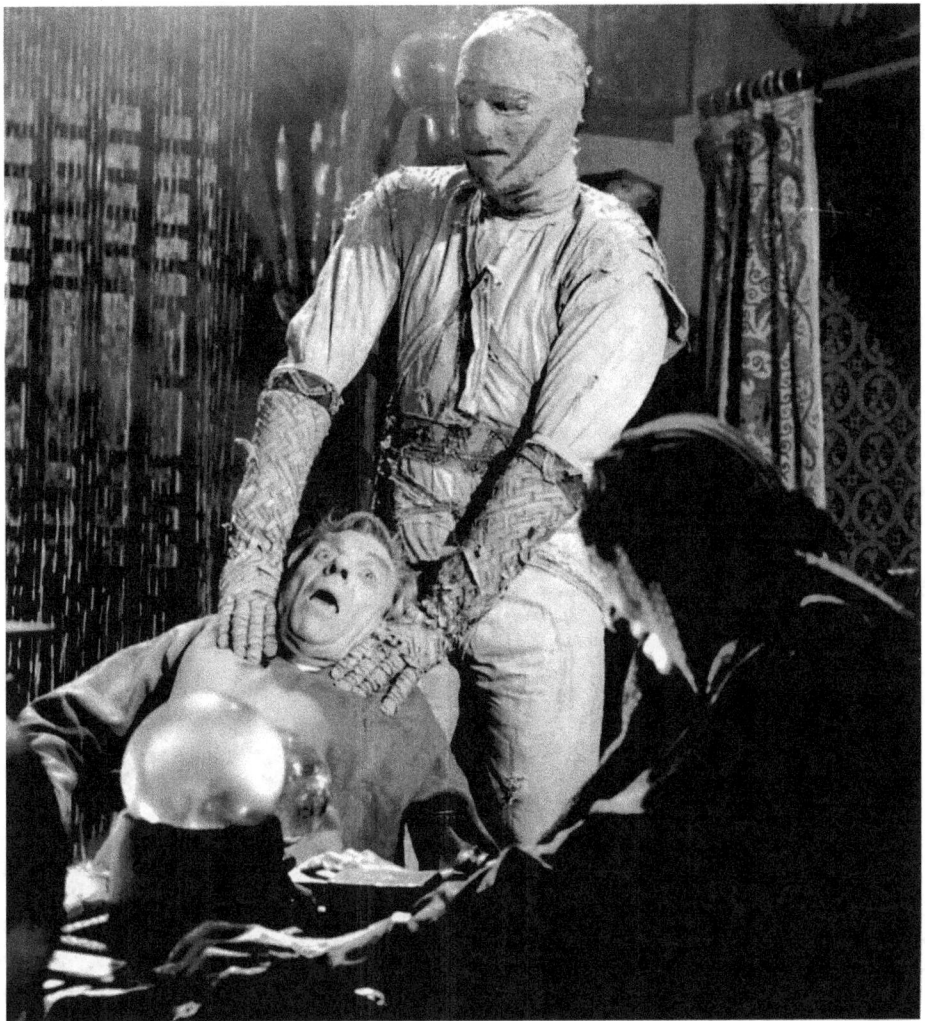

The mummy (Eddie Powell) kills Sir Basil as Haiti (Catherine Lacey) cackles.

charge of the investigation, is initially an insensitive detective but, after many deaths, he reveals his humane quality by telling the survivors to leave Egypt immediately. And then there is the pitiable and harassed Longbarrow whose meek subservience to Preston will eventually doom him. His fate is particularly sad because Preston, to satisfy his own ego, forces him to go on the search party and, consequently, become a victim of the curse.

The movie has its share of thrills. Prem's mummy looks somewhat different than the usual cinematic mummy, in part because the filmmakers based his appearance upon actual mummies in the Egyptian Rooms of the British Museum. He doesn't look as threatening as Christopher Lee's incarnation, though when he opens his crusty eyelids for the first time it is fearsome. This mummy is

Harry (Tim Barrett) tries to defend himself from the wrath of the mummy.

imaginative in his manner of disposing of those who dared to defile his master. He crushes one person's skull. He breaks a bottle of acid upon another victim. And he wraps another victim in a curtain and throws him out of the window. Prem's motivation for vengeance is devotion to his master. He is not evil but is only seeking justice against those whom he perceives as evildoers. In contrast, Hasmid has only hatred in his heart so his murderous actions are less excusable. And then there is Haiti whose cackle and accompanying glee at predicting deaths are quite chilling. Here is a woman who really enjoys her profession. Also adding to the film's excitement are the realistic fight scenes. Harry puts up a valiant defense against Prem and the climactic battle with the mummy against Paul, Claire and Inspector Barrani is quite thrilling.

As usual with Hammer Films, the entire cast of British actors approach their roles in a totally professional manner, with as much diligence and preparation as they would for a Shakespearean play. Andre Morell gives his customary fine performance as Sir Basil; through his expressions and tone, he makes it clear that he is seeking neither fame nor fortune but knowledge. John Phillips, with his disdainful tone and assumption of superiority, makes Preston totally despicable but he also skillfully conveys a trace of fear beneath the bluster. Elizabeth Sellars as Barbara doesn't have that much dialogue, but the camera often dwells on her expressions which adeptly transmit repressed emotions of hatred and resentment toward her husband. Maggie Kimberly as Claire has an exotic look that creates an air of mystery, which is appropriate for her enigmatic character. David Buck as Paul and Tim Barrett as Harry fulfill their requirements more than agreeably. Richard Delgado is perhaps a bit over-the-top as Hasmid but he is supposed to be a fanatic and fanatics by nature tend to be hysterical. Catherine Lacey's performance may be even more exaggerated but this makes Haiti truly frightening. However, with due respect to the other fine actors, it is Hammer regular Michael Ripper as Longbarrow who deserves special praise. He projects pitiable subservience not just by his words but by his perpetually obsequious

Sir Basil seeks only knowledge but suffers a horrible death.

Longbarrow (Michel Ripper) only wants to return to England but suffers an equally horrible death.

Italian poster for *The Mummy's Shroud*

manner. His eagerness to please the haughty Preston initially appears to reflect his character's timidity but it eventually becomes evident that he is hoping that his submission will get him back to his beloved England. When it seems that his wish will be granted, it is one of the few joyful moments in his life. This makes his subsequent disappointment and violent death truly lamentable. Ripper expertly creates a truly pathetic character.

This was the last film John Gilling directed for Hammer. He had begun writing scripts for Hammer in the late 1940s but left the studio after a quarrel with production chief Michael Carreras over authorship of a script in 1951. He returned in 1960 and directed his first film for the studio, *The Shadow of the Cat*. He subsequently directed a pair of swashbucklers, *The Pirates of Blood River* (1962) and *The Scarlet Blade* (1962), which were commercially successful. He wrote the screenplay for the horror film, *The Gorgon* (1964) and directed *The Reptile* (1966). He based his script for *The Mummy's Shroud* upon a story by John Elder (a pseudonym for Hammer's executive producer Anthony Hinds). Hammer considered him a good director but Kinsey's book reports that Gilling had "questionable

people skills" and that "his bad temper was legendary." Perhaps he was in a foul mood when he denounced the movie because it is better than he realized.

An atmospheric score by Don Banks is also an asset. Born in Australia, Banks established a reputation as a composer of concertos while also achieving fame as a jazz composer. He joined Hammer Studios in 1962 and subsequently scored eight films for the studio, either in the thriller or horror genre. This was his fourth score for a Gilling film, including one non-Hammer, and his last score for Hammer. The florid main theme, with a full chorus and orchestra, vividly recreates an ancient world.

The Mummy's Shroud doesn't deserve its terrible reputation. It should be remembered that the movie was designed to play the lower half of a double bill, underneath one of Hammer's more expensive features. It was produced for the express purpose of maintaining the interest of audiences while they awaited the main feature. *The Mummy's Shroud* fulfils this modest objective of being moderately entertaining and is a good B movie. There are certainly worse ways to spend 90 minutes. And it's difficult to not like a movie with the tagline: "Beware the beat of the cloth-wrapped feet."

Credits: Producer: Anthony Nelson Keys; Director: John Gilling; Screenplay: John Gilling, from an original story by John Elder; Cinematographer: Arthur Grant; Editor: Chris Barnes; Music: Don Banks; Special Effects: Les Bowie, Ian Scoones; Art Direction: Don Mingaye

Cast: Andre Morell (Sir Basil Walden); John Phillips (Stanley Preston); David Buck (Paul Preston); Elizabeth Sellars (Barbara Preston); Maggie Kimberley (Claire); Michael Ripper (Longbarrow); Tim Barrett (Harry); Richard Warner (Inspector Barrani); Roger Delgado (Hasmid); Catherine Lacey (Haiti); Dickie Owen (Prem); Bruno Barnabe (Pharaoh); Toni Gilpin (Pharaoh's wife); Toolsie Persaud (Kah-to-Bey); Eddie Powell (The Mummy); Andre Malandrinos (The Curator)

The Power

Professor James Tanner's days appear to be numbered. Someone is trying to kill him. But it isn't an ordinary man who wants to—quite literally—stop Jim Tanner's heart from beating. It is a man with an intellect far more advanced than any human being on earth. It is a man whose brain may be a hundred generations ahead of his contemporaries. It is a man with extraordinary paranormal and telekinetic capabilities. It is a man with the Power.

The Power (1968) was George Pal's penultimate production. Pal, an acknowledged master of science fiction and fantasy cinema, had a career which lasted more than four decades. He began his career in 1931 in Germany as an animator making cartoons and continued building his reputation in the Netherlands where he created "Puppetoons," short subjects which combined three-dimensional puppets with stop-motion animation. He came to the U.S. in 1939 and, due to his reputation, Paramount provided him with his own studio and a staff of talented assistants. From 1942 to 1948, he received seven Academy Award nominations for Best Short Subjects and, in 1944, received an Honorary Academy Award for "the development of novel techniques in the production of short subjects, known as Puppetoons." He continued making Puppetoons until interest diminished in the shorts and he started making full-length motion pictures.

From 1949 to 1975, George Pal produced 14 movies and the majority are in the science fiction and fantasy genres. His second film, *Destination Moon* (1950), is dated today but was a groundbreaking movie back when an actual moon-landing was nineteen years in the future. *When Worlds Collide* (1951) began his association with Paramount Pictures and won an Academy Award for special effects. *The War of the Worlds* (1953), based on the H. G. Wells novel, won another Academy Award for special effects and is a genuine science fiction classic; in 2011, the National Film Registry selected it as one of the "culturally, historically or aesthetically significant films" worthy of preservation. Pal moved to MGM and direct-

George Pal and George Barnes on the set of *The War of the Worlds*

ed as well as produced *tom thumb* (1958), which was a popular family movie and won another special effects Oscar. He returned to H. G. Wells for *The Time Machine* (1960), another box-office success and still another Oscar winner for special effects. *Atlantis, the Lost Continent* (1961) is undoubtedly his worst movie and damaged his reputation, despite the fact that the studio was responsible for its hurried production schedule. He bounced back with *The Wonderful World of the Brothers Grimm* (1962), which he filmed in the three-panel Cinerama process and was a critical as well as popular hit. Unfortunately, *The 7 Faces of Dr. Lao* (1964), despite good reviews and a nomination for special effects, failed at the box-office. In Hollywood, you are only as good as your last movie and Pal needed a successful film to

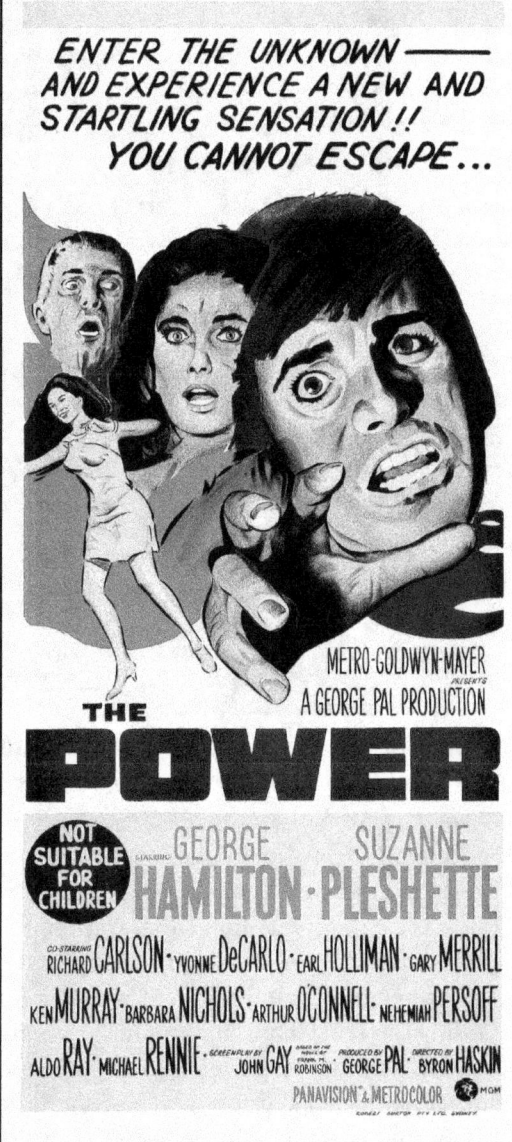

continue his career. He hoped that *The Power* would bring him that crucial success.

The Power is based upon the 1956 novel of the same title by Frank M. Robinson (1926-2014), an American science fiction and thriller author; he updated *The Power* in 2000 but the original version remains superior. Byron Haskin, who had directed the *The War of the Worlds* as well as *The Naked Jungle* (1954) and

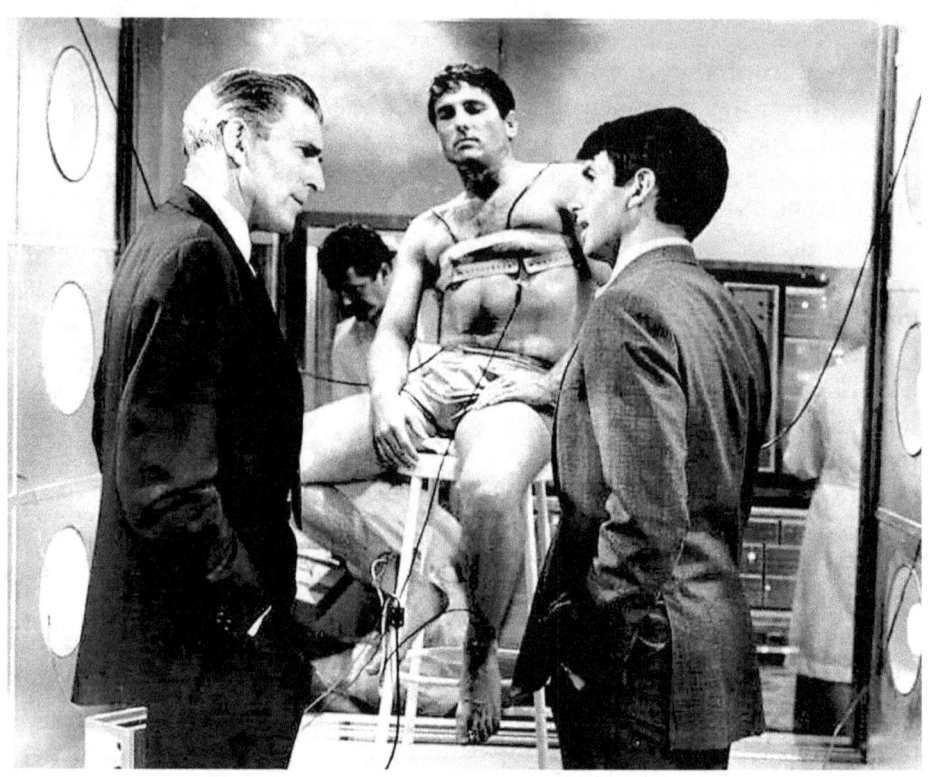

Professor James Tanner (George Hamilton) explains to Arthur Nordlund (Michael Rennie) the purpose of the research facility's experiments.

Conquest of Space (1955) for Pal, returned from semi-retirement to work with the producer for the fourth and last time on *The Power*. It is Pal's most underrated production as well as his most atypical. While it is a science fiction story, it unfolds as a mystery as Jim Tanner attempts to expose the identity of the superhuman killer before he becomes the next victim. It is somewhat Hitchcockian as Tanner is an innocent man trying to clear himself of a murder charge by finding the real villain. It contains an Agatha Christie-type element in that, one by one, possible suspects are dying in mysterious ways. And it is also a horror story as the killer's history reveals that he is willing to murder anyone, including his entire family, to achieve his nefarious goals.

At the beginning of the movie, Jim Tanner is a respected professor of biochemistry at a government research facility. He presides over a committee that is conducting experiments on the limits of endurance that humans can withstand to prepare them for space travel. Among the members of the committee are the chief of the institute Norman Van Zandt, geneticist Margery Lansing, biologist Talbot Scott, anthropologist Henry Hallson and physicist Carl Melnicker. Also present is the liaison from the U.S. government, Arthur Nordlund who has the authority to provide funding for the facility's research. During a meeting of the committee, Hallson is extremely anxious because of a questionnaire that he has submitted to all of the members who responded anonymously. The results indicate that one of the members possesses an exorbitantly superior intellect combined with paranormal powers. No one believes Hallson until he conducts an experiment that reveals that someone in the room is capable of telekinesis. When Hallson is later killed, he leaves a clue that may reveal the identity of his murderer. The clue is the name: Adam Hart.

The nightmare then begins for Jim Tanner. Police Lieutenant Corlane suspects Tanner of murdering Hallson. Van Zandt fires him because there is no record of his education and his history has been totally erased. Tanner determines that one of the committee members must be Adam Hart and that Hart is responsible for his loss of identity. After Sally Hallson tells Tanner that Hart was her husband's childhood friend, he travels to Hallson's hometown where he learns that Hart was born to a family of gypsies, all of whom died in a fire, though Adam survived. He interviews Hallson's parents and realizes Hart's lasting harmful impact upon them. He barely survives an attempt on his life by a garage mechanic who is under a compulsion to kill anyone inquiring about Hart. Back home, a mysterious crippling force repeatedly seizes Tanner and dangerously affects his heartbeat. He has strange visions that appear to exist only in his mind. With the help of Margery and Melnicker, Tanner narrows down his list of suspects. When he attempts to contact Van Zandt, he learns that the institute's chief has formed an alliance with other scientists to serve Hart in his plan to rule humanity. This leads to a near-fatal car crash for Tanner and his arrest by Corlane. He escapes and pursues the last two suspects until he exposes his adversary's identity which leads to a mental duel to the death and a startling surprise.

Tanner hallucinates under the control of the man with the Power.

John Gay's screenplay for *The Power* follows the basic plot of the novel, though he changes the names of some of the characters as well as the settings. The novel takes place at a university in Chicago while the film's institute is in Santa Marino, California; also, Joshua Flats in California replaces Brockton, South Dakota as Hallson's hometown. Gay successfully transmits some of Robinson's themes concerning the dangers that lurk in seemingly innocuous situations, from toy soldiers to street signs, from fun houses to merry-go-rounds. He also makes the killings more cinematic. In the novel, Hallson—called Olsen—dies of an unknown cause while sitting at his desk at his home; in the film, an invisible force attacks

Carl Melnicker (Nehemiah Persoff) suspects that Tanner is the man with the Power and tries to kill him.

him in his office and then kills him in a centrifuge. In the novel, when Tanner travels to Hallson's hometown, a farm boy tries to stab him to death; in the movie, the mechanic abandons him in the desert next to an Air Force gunnery range. These changes are obviously done to bring more action-oriented sequences to the film and are quite effective.

Other changes are more regrettable. The script eliminates a harrowing incident from the novel in which a concealed Hart almost succeeds in forcing

Tanner to drown himself. Missing from the film are frightening scenes in which Hart is a shadowy figure in the distance, always just out of Tanner's reach. Gay also simplifies Tanner's frantic attempts to evade Hart. In the novel, Tanner hides out in different flophouses at night, stays in crowded places during the day, takes stimulants to stay awake and becomes increasingly exhausted while he desperately tries to stay alive and expose Hart. Gay does not successfully translate this escalating fear and paranoia to the script; its inclusion would have increased the movie's suspense quotient.

The most obvious change is the ending in which Tanner exposes Nordlund as Hart and defeats him. In the novel, upon discovering that he also has the Power, Tanner is immediately corrupted by the knowledge; he cruelly commands Margery to kill Hart and then savors the idea of controlling the world. In the film, Tanner almost loses his battle with Hart until he discovers his own Power and is able to kill his enemy; he can then only wonder what effect his Power will have upon him before walking away with Margery. The film's ending is less cynical than the novel's and is arguably an improvement. This twist ending in both novel and film in which Tanner discovers that he has the Power may appear to be hackneyed but it explains why Nordlund was never able to kill Tanner the way he killed four other committee members.

The screenplay doesn't cheat. Prior to Nordlund's exposure as Adam Hart, the movie provides clues regarding Hart's identity. In the first scene, as Nordlund walks toward the research facility, he stops to look up at a large replica of the globe and smiles; he is pleased because he knows that the same world is his for the taking. During Hallson's experiment, Nordlund's surprised expression is because he realizes that someone else in the room also has the Power. Some critics wondered why Hallson didn't recognize Nordlund as Hart since they were friends in their adolescence but Hart's ability to affect people's memories explains this. In the novel, Hart can also affect the way that people see him.

Byron Haskin began directing in the silent era and then worked as a cinematographer and special effects coordinator. In 1939, he received a Technical Achievement Academy Award for developing the triple head background projector. As head of the

Michael Rennie smiles for a publicity photo.

Special Effects Department at Warner Bros. from 1937 to 1945, he received four Oscar nominations for Best Special Effects. He returned to directing in 1947 and subsequently proved to be reliable in virtually every genre, including Westerns, adventure, fantasy and film noir as well as science fiction. While his films appear to lack any kind of personal style, he still displayed a consistent craftsmanship. By the way, *The Naked Jungle*, the adventure movie about army ants that Haskin directed for Pal, introduced the word "marabunta"—which Haskin states that he created—to a generation. Other films that display his skill include: *Too Late for Tears* (1949), which in 2014 the Film Noir Foundation along with the UCLA Film & Television Archive restored; *Treasure Island* (1950), Walt Disney's first live-action film; *The Boss* (1956), a hard-hitting crime drama; *Robinson Crusoe on Mars* (1964), which didn't make much of an impact upon its release but has since acquired a considerable reputation.

(Note: In addition to his three notable science fiction movies for Pal and *Robinson Crusoe on Mars*, Haskin also directed *From the Earth to the Moon* in 1958 as well as six episodes of the television series, *The Outer Limits*, in 1963 and 1964; he was also an advisor and production associate on the pilot episode for *Star Trek* in 1966. However, in 1984 he stated that he never cared that much about science fiction and resented being typecast as a science fiction director: "It was a very difficult matter to bring yourself up to a completely dedicated belief in the material and unless you did, you were out of luck if you really wanted to make it believable." Despite what he may have thought in his later years, he certainly made his science fiction movies believable to millions of fans, excluding the awful *From the Earth to the Moon*.)

Haskin hadn't directed either a movie or a television episode for over four years and he was grateful to reunite with Pal for *The Power*, especially since he had read Robinson's novel upon its publication and found it fascinating. Though the film begins methodically as it introduces the characters and plot, it builds in intensity once the hunt begins. As Tanner investigates his former colleagues while simultaneously trying to expose Hart, the director reflects Tanner's escalating determination with an increasingly rapid pace. The tension is palpable throughout the film, especially in several marvelous set pieces. One of the most notable is the reality-twisting scene preceding Hallson's death in which the scientist is terrorized as doors and windows in his office disappear. The fight scene between Tanner and Melnicker in the kitchen is especially exciting. Also highly effective are the carousel and the firing range sequences, both of which almost result in Tanner's death. Then there is the hotel party scene and the stripper's teasing of a lifeless Melnicker which creates a queasy feeling not only for the stripper but within viewers. The final encounter in which Tanner confronts and battles Hart combines suspense with action and brings the film to a satisfying climax.

Pal and Haskin subsequently expressed some misgivings about the screenplay. In 1977, Pal told Gail Morgan Hickman: "I wish we would have stuck closer to the book. I'm disappointed with the way it turned out. John Gay is a very fine writer, but I think he wrote too much away from the book." In 1975, Haskin told Graham Shirley: "I came into the show when it was fully prepared. I assisted John Gay in polishing one or two points, but I had no authority to change anything further; I felt that a few things could have been changed but I didn't go into it because I was glad to be working again." In 1984, he told Joe Adamson: "I was trying in every way to put weird supernatural notes into the chase to duplicate the way I subconsciously remembered the book affecting me. The screenplay didn't have anything of that sort." Regarding the theme of Tanner's loss of identity: "That was the thing I phased in powerfully; Gay had it in there, but I stressed it and made a point of it, made the scenes about it bigger."

John Gay, who has quite an impressive resumé, would probably not object to criticism of his screenplay. In his autobiography, *Any Way I Can: 50 Years in Show Business* (Bear Manor; 2009), Gay mentions the movie very briefly: "Two screenplays followed, one a supernatural story, *The Power*, in a milieu in which I don't feel comfortable, proven by lukewarm reviews." It appears that Gay, who was the recipient of an Academy Award nomination for co-writing *Separate Tables* (1958) and won a Writers Guild Laurel Award for Television Lifetime Achievement, may not have been the most suit-

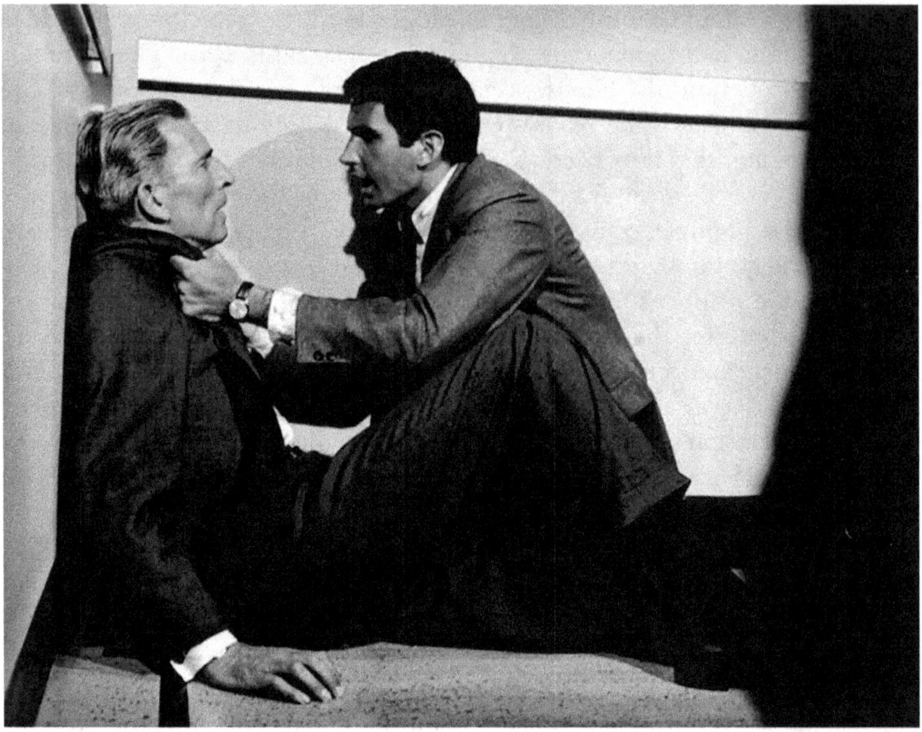

Tanner frantically tries to revive Nordlund (Michael Rennie) who has seemingly been attacked by the man with the Power.

able writer to adapt the novel. Nevertheless, the script's assets outnumber its deficiencies. Significantly, the horrific basic theme of the novel remains intact. In addition to showing the destructive effects that a superior mind can have upon ordinary human beings, the film subtly suggests the effects that Hart's powers would have upon the future of the human race. This is what frightens Hallson so much. This is why Van Zandt and Scott are willing to accept Hart as their master.

Tanner and Marjorie (Suzanne Pleshette) look down upon the centrifuge.

George Pal reportedly didn't want George Hamilton to star in the film but MGM executives insisted on him. Regardless, Hamilton is excellent as Jim Tanner. As the center of the film, Hamilton displays the sincerity that grounds the fantastic story in reality. He is believable as a dedicated scientist, as a determined detective, as a frightened man on the run for his life and as a man with newly discovered superpowers. He is especially convincing registering panic and terror when an unseen Hart exerts pressure upon his heart as well as his brain. Suzanne Pleshette registers nicely as Margery Lansing, Tanner's colleague and romantic interest. All of the co-stars bring authority to their roles, but Michael Rennie as Arthur Nordlund stands out due in part to the significance of his role but also due to his strong screen presence. Incidentally, it is gratifying to see Rennie and Richard Carlson, two recognizable icons of 1950s science-fiction movies, together in one film. Carlson plays Norman Van Zandt with his usual earnest commitment while Arthur O'Connell also makes a strong impression as Henry Hallson. But all of the supporting actors provide forceful performances that add to the movie's success.

Nordlund tries to escape from his adversary who is more powerful than he is.

Miklos Rozsa's superb score for *The Power* is another asset to the film. Rozsa uses the cimbalom prominently in the score. The cimbalom is an instrument that is popular in central European countries, including Hungary, which is Rozsa's—and George Pal's—birthplace. In his autobiography, *Double Life* (Wynwood Press; 1998), Rozsa writes: "I was fond of George Pal, for he was an amiable and charming gentleman. Since the main character in the film was a gypsy, he wanted me to use a cimbalom. A cimbalom is a sort of large zither played with hammers, which produces a very distinctive sound, something between a badly tuned piano and a broken-down harpsichord. I don't like the instrument much, but I didn't object because it seemed appropriate for the character of the man." Rozsa utilizes the cimbalom primarily to signify either Adam Hart's presence or his lethal impact upon others. The composer cleverly provides another clue concerning Nordlund's real identity when Nordlund appears to suffer the same kind of crippling attack that killed Hallson and almost killed Tanner; as he clutches his heart and struggles to reach safety, Hart's theme again plays on the soundtrack—but *without* the cimbalom.

It is interesting that director Haskin, perhaps at Pal's request, gives the cimbalom a cameo role in the movie. He interrupts the opening credits to show a musician's hands playing the cimbalom and again during the final confrontation between Tanner and Hart. But the most jarring use of the cimbalom occurs in the middle of the film during the convention scene. Tanner, Margery and Melnicker have joined a group of conventioneers at a hotel to escape

Hart's influence. In the midst of the gaiety, Tanner senses Hart's presence as he nervously walks through the lobby. This feeling intensifies as Hart's theme begins playing, apparently on the soundtrack. But then Tanner is startled to see a band with one of the musicians playing the cimbalom. Suddenly the soundtrack music becomes diegetic music that is actually a part of the story. This revelation adds a surreal element to the movie that is disturbing. Since it is Hart's theme that is playing, it is as though Adam Hart has taken control of the movie as well as the characters. Supporting this is the fact that Hart came from a family of gypsies and the band members are dressed as gypsies. This raises the question of whether they are real or if Hart is nearby and has planted them in Tanner's mind. The fact that Melnicker does not leave the party alive strengthens this possibility.

On the liner notes for the 1978 Citadel LP entitled *Film Music—Miklos Rozsa*, which contains the soundtrack to *The Power*, Tony Thomas writes: "*The Power* offered a generous amount of murder, mayhem and suspense but left viewers wondering what it was all about. Among those left wondering was the man hired to write the score. Dr. Rozsa claims that he still does not fully understand the picture. Nevertheless, it did not stop him from writing music of excitement and intrigue with brilliant musical colors." With all due respect to Mr. Thomas, many viewers knew exactly what it was all about.

Some authors of reference books also appear to have misunderstood the movie. In *The Films of George Pal* (A.S. Barnes; 1977), Gail Morgan Hickman writes: "It is disappointing that the film did not turn out better; it is one of Pal's minor productions, an interesting, competent film not up to the standards we have come to expect from Pal." In *The Great Science Fiction Pictures* by James Robert Parish and Michael Pitts (Scarecrow Press; 1977), the authors write that the movie "is one of those ambitious projects that did not jell, despite a competent script, a capable cast, excellent special effects and a well-mounted production."

Other authors are more perceptive. Phil Hardy in *Science Fiction: The Film Encyclopedia* (William Morrow; 1984) calls it a "taut para-psychological thriller." In *Things to Come* (Times Books; 1977), Douglas Menville and R. Reginald write: "*The Power* vanished without a trace soon after being released but it deserves a second look. Rising above its hackneyed spy plot, it makes some significant points about the effects of real power on those who wield it: even the greatest among us is susceptible. This is a minor classic." In *A Pictorial History of Science Fiction Films* (Citadel Press; 1975), Jeff Rovin writes: "The film is a mature, terrifying production that deserved much better distribution than it received; abetted by an inventive score, superlative special effects and a lively pace, the film is an entertaining, constantly surprising science fiction classic."

John Brosnan appears to have had second thoughts about the movie. In *Future Tense: The Cinema of Science Fiction* (St. Martin's Press; 1978), Brosnan writes: "It is a fairly interesting adaptation of a minor novel; though the script

French poster for *The Power*

is disjointed and the film rather sluggish in places, it is not a complete failure." However, in *The Science Fiction Encyclopedia* (Doubleday; 1979), Brosnan calls it "a tightly plotted story of a mutant supermind masquerading as an ordinary human being; it has an interesting script and taut direction that led to one critic calling it one of the finest sf films."

The one critic that Brosnan is referring to is John Baxter. In *Science Fiction in the Cinema* (Paperback Library; 1970), Baxter writes: "Among the expensively mounted sf films of the Sixties, those less extravagant tended to be lost, a fate that befell the most penetrating of all the Pal/Haskin collaborations. It is one of the finest of all sf films, a tightly wound thriller that comes close to combining the optimism of science fiction with the pragmatism of the cinema. Bound together by Miklos Rozsa's clever score, it gains from an inventive script and performances of remarkable integrity. One admits the plot faults of this remarkable film without once denying its substantial status as fantasy and cinema." (Note: Brosnan and Baxter, fellow Australians, also wrote fiction and co-authored the 1986 horror novel *Torched!* under the pseudonym of James Blackstone.)

The Power was a failure at the box-office. Domestic theatrical rentals were less than $1,000,000 which was disastrous as far as Pal's future prospects were concerned. He subsequently found it increasingly difficult to interest studios in future projects, perhaps due in part to MGM's dismissal of its veteran workers, as recalled by the film's director. In the book, *Byron Haskin: Interviewed by Joe Adamson—A Directors Guild of America Oral History* (Scarecrow Press; 1984), Haskin states that, while he was making the movie, the management at MGM was purging the studio to make way for the so-called new wave of filmmakers: "That meant that all the old-timers, all the experienced personnel, the expert staff that MGM had spent years and fortunes assembling had to go; I knew the end was near." After completing this movie, Haskin was happy to permanently retire. In an interview with Graham Shirley for the Australian film magazine, *Cinema Papers* (March-April 1975 issue), Haskin expressed his opinion on the movie's box-office failure: "The personal friction between MGM and George Pal—the hatred between them you just wouldn't believe—was allowed to operate on that film's economy. It wasn't released with any fanfare. It was grudgingly left to escape with everybody at MGM hoping it would flop because they were trying to get rid of Pal."

However, Gail Morgan Hickman states that Pal remained at MGM for two more years while he hoped to make a film version of *Logan's Run*, a property that he had been nurturing ever since he read the novel prior to publication

and while he was making *The Power*. After the studio cancelled the project for the third time, he bitterly left the studio. (MGM eventually filmed it in 1975 without Pal, which was very disheartening to him.) After several years of further disappointments, Warner Bros. approved his proposal for *Doc Savage: Man of Bronze* (1975), based upon the popular series of pulp novels. Unfortunately, the movie was a box-office disaster and ended his career. Despite his estimable history of many successful movies, he was unable to achieve funding for any additional film projects and Hollywood discarded him.

The Power was one of the first major films to depict telekinesis. It achieves its impact without exploding heads or blood-splattered body parts. Its impact is more subtle. In the film's closing scene, Tanner and Margery stand before a large replica of the globe and it is obvious that Tanner is contemplating what he can achieve with his Power, whether good or evil. There have since been numerous movies about the subject, including *Carrie* (1976), *The Fury* (1978) and *Scanners* (1981). Only *The Medusa Touch* similarly suggests—and actually depicts—the impact upon the entire world that a single person with such paranormal powers could have.

The Power is an exciting, suspenseful and provocative movie. It deserves to stand alongside the more renowned films of George Pal, one of the true maestros of fantasy and science fiction cinema.

Credits: Producer: George Pal; Director: Byron Haskin; Screenwriter: John Gay, based upon the novel by Frank M. Robinson; Cinematographer: Ellsworth Fredericks; Editor: Thomas McCarthy; Music: Miklos Rozsa; Special Visual effects: J. McMillan Johnson, Gene Warren; Art Direction: Alfred W. Davis, Merryll Pye; Set Decoration: Henry Grace, Don Greenwood, Jr.

Cast: George Hamilton (Jim Tanner); Suzanne Pleshette (Margery Lansing); Michael Rennie (Arthur Nordlund); Richard Carlson (Norman Van Zandt); Earl Holliman (Talbot Scott); Arthur O'Connell (Henry Hallson); Nehemiah Persoff (Carl Melnicker); Gary Merrill (Lieutenant Corlane); Aldo Ray (Mechanic); Yvonne DeCarlo (Sally Hallson); Ken Murray (Grover); BarbaraNichols (Flora); Vaughn Taylor (Mr. Hallson); Celia Lovsky (Mrs. Hallson); Miiko Taka (Mrs. Van Zandt); Beverly Hills (Stripper)

Journey to the Far Side of the Sun aka Doppelgänger

Journey to the Far Side of the Sun (1969), titled *Doppelgänger* in the United Kingdom, is a science fiction film that failed at the box-office and received mostly negative reviews. It was the first live-action film produced by the husband-and-wife team of Gerry and Sylvia Anderson. It was also their first attempt to produce entertainment for adults. The Andersons had achieved fame for their children's television series featuring marionettes such as *Thunderbirds*, *Stingray* and *Captain Scarlet and the Mysterons* which were very popular in the U.K. throughout the 1960s. They also made two feature films in the '60s based on the *Thunderbirds* series.

The Andersons had been hoping for several years for an opportunity to make a theatrical movie with actors instead of puppets. Actually, Gerry had directed a low-budget movie in 1960, *Crossroads to Crime*, which did nothing to advance his career; Sylvia was a production assistant on the film. In 1968, Universal Pictures finally gave the Andersons their long-awaited opportunity. The Hollywood-based studio had recently established an office in London and Universal executive Jay Kanter was actively looking for new projects. Gerry met with Kanter and proposed *Doppelgänger*, a story that he and Sylvia had written years before for a possible television production. Kanter approved, assuming a suitable script could be written. Gerry and Sylvia quickly completed a script with the assistance of Donald James. Filming took place from July to October 1968 at England's Pinewood studios and at the film production facilities in the Algarve, Portugal.

(Note: Gerry and Sylvia Anderson married in 1960 and divorced in 1981. Their respective duties during their partnership might give an indication about the production of *Doppelgänger*. In 1991, Sylvia stated: "Generally speaking, there was a division of labor whereby I would create the characters and Gerry would devise the action sequences of the plot; the storyline was a blend of the two." In 1996, Gerry stated: "Reg Hill [the art director] was the second in command and the press should have focused on him and me but they couldn't resist the husband-and-wife angle and a woman makes a more saleable picture." With these words, Gerry seems to be downplaying Sylvia's involvement, but he wrote this several years after their bitter divorce. Regarding that divorce, Sylvia wrote: "Gerry could still not accept that I was newsworthy in my own right and shared the limelight with him." Acrimonious relationships are not the subject of this chapter. Based upon their prior achievements, they probably deserve equal credit for *Doppelgänger*.)

Universal released *Doppelgänger* in England in October 1969 and in the United States the following month. Studio executives requested a title change for the U.S. release and decided upon *Journey to the far Side of the Sun*. Prior to the film's release, *Variety*'s review was overly nitpicking: "Despite some of the finest and most imaginative special effects and sharp production values, the film is so burdened with confusing elements that it frequently fails to make sense." Upon its opening in neighborhood theaters in New York City, Howard Thompson in *The New York Times* was more positive, if guarded: "The scientific theory and plot twist is so original and intriguing that it rates a larger movie, at least one with more stratospheric sweep and suspense."

The movie appeared in theaters the year after the critical and commercial successes of two major science fiction films, *2001: A Space Odyssey* and *Planet of the Apes*, and it was compared unfavorably to those two blockbusters. But the Andersons only had a fraction of their budget and had more modest ambitions. They were intent only on proving that they could make an intelligent science fiction movie for adult audiences. The movie's box-office disappointment on both sides of the Atlantic would appear to

Astronaut Glenn Ross (Roy Thinnes) and Public Relations representative Paolo Landi (Franco De Rosa).

indicate that they failed. But the passage of time often allows for a more impartial judgement of a movie. While it has its share of flaws, it is inventive and memorable. In essence, it generates a sense of wonder, the ultimate objective of all good science fiction.

The setting of *Journey to the Far Side of the Sun* is Portugal in the 21st century. British scientists at the European Space Exploration Complex (EUROSEC) have discovered another planet in the solar system rotating in the same orbit as earth's but at the exact opposite side of the sun. When Dr. Hassler, an enemy agent, steals information about the discovery, EUROSEC chief Jason Webb accelerates a voyage to the planet. Because the British government is reluctant to fund the exploration, Webb requests the aid of the United States from the National Aeronautics Space Administration (NASA) liaison. NASA will finance the project but only if their foremost astronaut Glenn Ross can command the spaceship, which is called the *Phoenix*. After Webb agrees, Ross assists in training British astrophysicist John Kane to prepare for space travel and to be his co-pilot. Ross is also having personal problems, specifically a contentious relationship with his wife Sharon who blames him for his sterility while he accuses her of infidelity.

The round trip to the new planet is scheduled to last six weeks and the launch is successful. When they awaken from hibernation, Ross and Kane leave the *Phoenix* in a shuttle to explore the new planet. But the shuttle crashes and Kane is critically injured. Upon awakening, Ross is shocked to see Webb who tells him that he must have reversed the course of the *Phoenix* because only three weeks have passed. When Ross denies turning back, officials suspect him of deliberately aborting the mission. He becomes increasingly confused as he discovers that everything in his home is reversed, from the position of light switches to the lettering on containers. He eventually tells Webb that he believes that he didn't land back on his Earth but on the planet that was his destination, a parallel world which is a mirror image of earth and on which everything and everyone duplicated but reversed. This includes Webb, whom he claims is not the Webb that he knew back on his earth. He adds that while he is on this mirror planet, his duplicate is on the opposite planet undergoing the same lemma. Webb, who has just learned that the organs in Kane's body are reversed, believes that Ross' theory is the only logical answer to his own bewildering questions.

They decide that Ross must command another shuttle but with the controls and the polari-

Above: Physicist John Kane (Ian Hendry) enters the space shuttle that will take him and Ross to the rocketship.

Below: After the shuttle crashes, Ross emerges from the wreckage unharmed but Kane is unconscious.

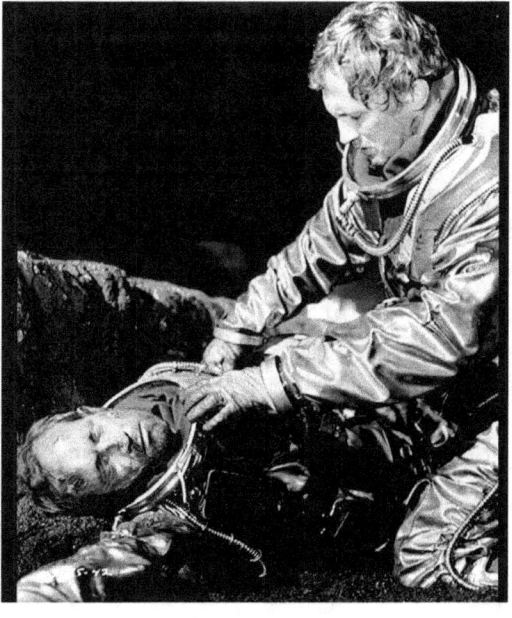

Science Fiction Thrills...Horror Chills

Italian lobby card

ty of the electrical systems reversed. They name the shuttle the *Doppelgänger*, which Ross will pilot to merge with the *Phoenix* before returning to his earth. They assume that his duplicate will be doing the same thing simultaneously, only returning to the duplicate Earth. The shuttle successfully launches but Ross is unable to reunite with the orbiting *Phoenix* because of the reverse polarity. Losing control, he crashes into the EUROSEC Complex, killing himself and destroying the entire facility, including all the records of his exploration and discovery. This same catastrophe has apparently happened on both planets. The only survivor is Webb—presumably, both Webbs on their respective planets—who, years later, is confined to an institution for his mental as well as his physical condition. As he stares at his reflection in a mirror, he accelerates his wheelchair and crashes into the mirror and, symbolically, into his duplicate self. He has become totally deranged because no one believes his story of a duplicate world.

Conflicts between the producers and the director plagued the production of *Doppelgänger*. In the book, *Gerry Anderson: the Authorized Biography* (Legend Books; 1996) by Simon Archer and Stan Nicholls, the authors report Gerry's side of the ensuing conflict. One of Jay Kanter's stipulations for approving the production was that an established director had to sign on. When Robert Parrish became available, Kanter insisted that he direct the movie. Gerry states that he regularly allowed his directors the freedom to interpret scripts in their own way, but he was still accustomed to being in charge. Parrish quickly demonstrated that he had his own ideas that extended beyond directing. For instance, he deleted some scenes without consulting with the producers. When Gerry demanded their inclusion, the director filmed them under protest. The relationship between producers and director grew increasingly unpleasant during the course of filming. In her autobiography, *Yes, M'Lady* (Smith Gryphon; 1991), Sylvia only mentions that "it was our first big-budget film and was directed by Hollywood veteran Robert Parrish" with no criticism of him. However, in a 1992 interview for *Time Screen: The Magazine of British Telefantasy*, Sylvia stated: "I don't think that Parrish was a brilliant choice. I think his direction was uninspired. We had a lot of trouble getting what we wanted from him."

It should be noted that Parrish had a lengthy and distinguished film career. He began as a child actor during the silent era and then became an editor in the early 1940s. He won an Academy Award for co-editing *Body and Soul* (1947) and was nominated again for *All the King's Men* (1950). He directed his first film in 1951, a crime story entitled *Cry Danger*, which the Film Noir Foundation and the UCLA Film and Television Archive restored in 2011. He received acclaim for *The Purple Plain* (1955), a World War II drama which was nominated for a BAFTA Award for Best British Film. Among his other movies are the Western, *The Wonderful Country* (1959), and the romantic drama, *In the French Style* (1963).

Italian lobby card

Sharon Ross (Lynn Loring) tells Lisa Hartman (Loni von Friedl) and security chief Neumann (George Sewel) about her husband's strange behavior.

Regarding his only science fiction film, Parrish chose not to tell his side of the story, at least not publicly. He wrote two books of memoirs, *Growing Up in Hollywood* (Harcourt; 1976) and *Hollywood Doesn't Live Here Anymore* (Little, Brown; 1998) but, though he discusses many of his films in the second book, he doesn't mention the Andersons or their movie. Perhaps he just wanted to forget it.

In actuality, Parrish had far more filmmaking experience—with human beings—than the Andersons and this may be why Jay Kanter insisted that he direct the movie. In his best films, Parrish tended to focus on character development. As an editor, he also had some knowledge of how to reduce needless exposition. A relationship of mutual respect between him and the Andersons would have been beneficial to the film's development. Due perhaps to their inability to work together, the first third of the film depicting the preparation for the launch moves at a slow pace, due in part to the script's emphasis on scientific details. Unquestionably, the script should have focused less on technology and more on the features of the new planet. It would be fascinating to see additional examples of the planet's reversal of familiar objects and places. More interactions of Ross with his duplicate wife would be equally interesting, along with his possible romance with EUROSEC executive Lisa Hartman, actually her double. While the script may have been making the argument that the enormity of the scientific discovery makes these human

Gerry and Sylvia Anderson (middle) wrote the "Earthbound" episode of *Space 1999*, shown here with guest star Christopher Lee (seated) and series regular Barbara Bain (right).

problems seem petty by comparison, this point is obscure. If the producers had given Parrish more freedom, he might have clarified both the human and the scientific themes.

But to give the Andersons their deserved credit, they wrote the original story which is the foundation for the movie. The script's fantastic premise of the earth and its mirror planet is a prime example of speculative fiction. The complications of Ross trying to re-adjust to his home planet without realizing that it is a different planet are engrossing, especially since the viewer at this point is as puzzled as Ross. This is especially intriguing when it is understood that the Ross who is trying to re-adjust to his home life has never known the Sharon that he is trying to reunite with. Ideally, the Andersons should have further expounded on this dilemma. Nevertheless, one of the highlights of the movie is the pivotal scene in which Ross and Webb agree on their seemingly bizarre theory and strengthen their agreement by shaking hands. The fact that this triumphant scene is followed by tragedy only highlights its significance. It is sad that the hope and promise of the early scenes lead to such a depressing finale but that is part of what makes the film memorable.

Of course, the depiction of a parallel universe in the media did not originate with the Andersons. It is quite possible that Gerry or Sylvia or both saw the 1960 episode of *The Twilight Zone* titled "Mirror Image" or the 1963 episode titled "The Parallel," either of which might have generated the idea for *Doppelgänger*. Rod Serling wrote both episodes and it is tantalizing to think what Serling could have done if he had re-written the Andersons' script. Incidentally, Robert Parrish directed three episodes of *The Twilight Zone*, including the memorable "A Stop at Willoughby" in 1960; Serling wrote all three.

In addition to the friction between the Andersons and Parrish, other problems hindered the production. Due to a disagreement over how to shoot scenes inside the space shuttle, Gerry Anderson's friendship with cinematographer and long-time collaborator John Read ended in bitterness. Union demands created another problem. Visual effects director Derek Meddings had supervised the construction of an expertly crafted space shuttle which was transported to Pinewood studios. But the film carpenters' union at Pinewood insisted that they had to build all the models to be used in the film. Consequently, the model was destroyed and the union built an inferior replica. Additionally, one of the 6-foot models of a rocketship caught fire, was severely damaged and had to be quickly rebuilt. Adding further aggravation, location filming in Portugal had to be terminated in September when the country's prime minister was deposed. Concerned that a coup might occur, the film crew had to quickly leave the country.

Derek Meddings' special effects are outstanding. The film reportedly contains more than two hundred effects shots, including futuristic automobiles and dwellings which are quite convincing. The launching of the *Phoenix* featured such authentic models that many people assumed that library footage of actual launches was used. The voyaging of the ship through space is almost poetic in its beauty. The spectacular crash that climaxes the film is awesome in its destructiveness and is so realistic that it validates the use of miniatures over today's reliance of computer-generated effects.

The shuttle, named the *Doppelgänger* will hopefully take Ross back to the *Phoenix* to begin his return trip home.

The rocketship, called the *Phoenix*, blasts off on the journey to the newly-discovered planet.

All of the actors are persuasive in their roles. Roy Thinnes is totally credible as Ross and is especially impressive during the extended sequence in which he gradually comprehends the only theory that fits the facts. Ian Hendry is equally believable as Kane and likeable enough that his character's death, though necessary, leaves a void in the story. Patrick Wymark as Webb stands out in part because of his determined desperation to advance scientific knowledge regardless of the financial or human cost; his despondent expression at the finale is heartrending, particularly since his caretakers probably consider him delusional. Lynn Loring is also good as Sharon, plausibly displaying contempt for her husband because she believes that he considers his profession more important than their marriage. Loring, who was married to Thinnes at the time, signed for the role just prior to the start of filming

Ross is confused that everything is reversed.

Science Fiction Thrills...Horror Chills *141*

Italian lobby card

after the original actress, Gayle Hunnicutt, became ill. The always-reliable Herbert Lom makes a brief but notable impression as Dr. Hassler.

Journey to the Far Side of the Sun contains some interesting ideas. Beneath the main narrative is a bleak implication that attacks the core of human existence. This establishes the sense of wonder that is manifested within the film. Many movies have shown that human beings are not alone in the universe and that they share the vast regions of outer space with interplanetary aliens. But this film shows that they share their own solar system with a duplication, or reflection, of themselves. And this is frightening because it means that there is nothing unique about the earth, its nations, its histories and the individual personalities of every human being inhabiting the earth.

Taking this a step further, can humans claim to have free will when their duplicates are doing the exact same thing as they are at the exact same time? If they don't have free will, then perhaps they are controlled by some mystical power existing within the sun to which both earths are bound by gravity. Such ideas were popular centuries ago when ancient civilizations worshipped the sun and believed in a deity existing within it. Perhaps these primitive ancestors were correct. The idea that interplanetary travel might validate primeval superstition is humbling to the conceit of humanity.

Then again, if a duplicate earth exists, there could conceivably be triplicate or quadruplicate or quintuplicate earths somewhere out there orbiting other stars within other solar systems. Perhaps because they are in other solar

systems, they are not reflections but are actually earths in different stages of development. For instance, the triplicate earth might be a hundred years ahead of the development of this earth while the quadruplicate may be a hundred years behind it. Then again, the quintuplicate earth may be a thousand years ahead of it. It is conceivable that some kind of supreme being or master ma-

Ross and Kane prepare for their trip aboard the Phoenix to the far side of the sun.

nipulator is controlling the development of these earths. Perhaps this supremacy, whether benevolent or malevolent, is experimenting with human beings in a manner similar to the way human beings experiment with animals.

Journey to the Far Side of the Sun is the kind of movie that provokes such fantastic interpretations and philosophical analysis. And, suffice to say, it also provokes pompous discussion. In the final analysis, this movie may just be an exciting adventure about the exploration of space—nothing more, nothing less. So perhaps it is best to just sit back and enjoy it—or not.

Most reference books tend to criticize the movie. In *Science Fiction: The Film Encyclopedia* (William Morrow; 1984), Phil Hardy calls it "lackluster with a wooden, overtalkative script and erratic storyline that drains the movie of all possible drama." In *The Great Science Fiction Pictures* (Scarecrow Press; 1977), James Robert Parrish and Michael R. Pitts write: "A faltering script and listless production values mitigate against the film's success." In *Things To Come* (Times Books; 1977), Douglas Menville and R. Reginald write: "Although the story line is just so much hokum, the special effects make it worth a single viewing." In *A Pictorial History of Science Fiction Films* (Citadel; 1975), Jeff Rovin calls it "a confusing but colorful story with superb special effects." John Brosnan in *Future Tense: The Cinema of Science Fiction* (St. Martin's; 1978) praises the superior special effects but writes: "The Andersons lose control of the plot and the film degenerates into pure confusion (while) the script is a mixture of pseudo-science at its most illogical and sheer pretentiousness." In *The Science Fiction Encyclopedia* (Doubleday; 1979), Brosnan partially revises his opinion: "The film is an above average offering from the Anderson production team; no doubt the credit lies with the direction of Robert Parrish who handles the confused and illogical plot with style." Brosnan then curiously adds: "The confusions of the plot are compounded by the fact that the story is told in flashbacks by a character in a mental asylum, giving a Dr. Caligari-like ambiguity to the whole film."

(Note: This is the only reference work that mentions a flashback version of the film. Gerry Anderson's biography does not refer to such a version and neither does Sylvia in her autobiography. Perhaps this version was released on the duplicate earth and the duplicate Brosnan saw it there!)

Most of the criticism seems to be directed at the film's premise of a mirror planet. The concept of another planet on the other side of the sun is obviously illogical. Basic astronomy explains that the earth is influenced to some degree by other planets in the solar system. Due to gravitational effects, the presence of an additional planet would have a further impact on the earth and the cause of this impact would be identified by probes or other scientific means. This is actually how and why the EUROSEC unmanned satellite discovers the new planet. Quibblers complained that such a mysterious gravitational pull would have been detected long ago. But the movie is science *fiction*, not science *fact*. Once you accept the premise, despite its invalidity, there is nothing confusing about all that follows.

Due to its commercial failure, Gerry and Sylvia Anderson didn't make any more theatrical features but they continued working in the science fiction genre on television with the series, *UFO* and *Space: 1999*. Nevertheless, though *Journey to the Far Side of the Sun* is not a great movie, it is a very good one. And it has a sense of wonder.

By the way, how about an octuplicate earth?

Or a decuplicate earth?

Or...?

Credits: Executive Producers: Lew Grade, Jay Kanter; Producers: Gerry Anderson, Sylvia Anderson; Director: Robert Parrish; Screenwriters: Gerry Anderson, Sylvia Anderson, Donald James, based on a story by Gerry Anderson and Sylvia Anderson; Cinematographer: John Read; Editor: Len Walker; Special Effects: Norman Foster; Visual Effects Director: Derek Meddings; Music: Barry Gray; Art Direction: Bob Bell

Cast: Roy Thinnes (Glenn Ross); Ian Hendry (John Kane); Patrick Wymark (Jason Webb); Lynn Loring (Sharon Ross); Herbert Lom (Dr. Hassler); Loni von Friedl (Lisa Hartman); George Sewell (Mark Neumann); Edward Bishop (David Poulson, NASA Liaison); Franco Derosa (Paulo Landi); Vladek Sheybal (Psychiatrist); Philp Madoc (Dr. Pontini); George Mikel (Captain Ross); Cy Grant (Dr. Gordon); Peter van Dissel (Mallory); Annette Kerr (Nurse)

Brain Drainers: The Groundstar Conspiracy & Who?

In the early 1970s, two movies with similar themes were released. *The Groundstar Conspiracy* (1972) and *Who?* (1974) are both based upon futuristic novels and involve political espionage with science fictional trappings. Both movies concern a character who has been in a serious accident that has disfigured him. These two persons also receive extensive surgical procedures. Upon recovery, they both claim to have some degree of amnesia. They are both subjected to intense scrutiny by authorities who attempt to find out who they really are, particularly whether or not they are foreign agents. And, in both films, a tenacious intelligence operative is determined to discover the truth about these mysterious individuals. An examination of both movies will illustrate not only their similarities and differences but, most of all, their individual uniqueness.

The basis of *The Groundstar Conspiracy* is the 1966 novel, *The Alien* by L. P. Davies (1914-1988), a British author of science fiction novels. Since Davies also wrote mystery novels, *The Alien* combines these two genres for an intriguing plot. The setting of the novel is England in 2016, 50 years in the future. Sci-

entists and military officials conduct an emergency meeting to discuss a hospital patient with amnesia. His name is John Maxwell, and he has strange characteristics. In addition to unusual skin and hair, the liquid flowing through his veins doesn't appear to be blood. The chief intelligence operative, Gregory Tuxan, provides information indicating that Maxwell came into existence in January 2015 with no traceable record of him prior to that time. However, Maxwell also has a connection to the Glyderbank Research Establishment, a covert government facility that was destroyed by an explosion due to sabotage. There is also the report of the landing of an Unidentified Flying Object near an isolated village in December 2014. According to

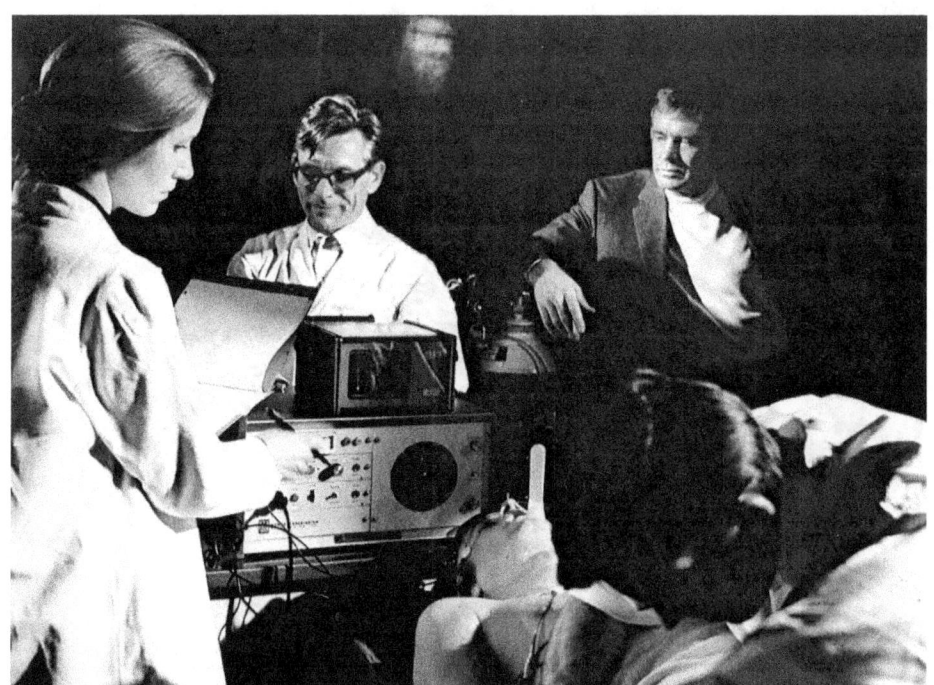

Dr. Plover (Anna Hagan), her assistant and Tuxan (George Peppard) observe the unconscious patient (Michael Sarrazin); this scene is not in the movie.

a farmer, several mysterious beings disembarked from the UFO. Furthermore, Maxwell believes that he doesn't belong in this world. A hospital nurse, Kaylee, is one of the few people who displays sympathy for his plight. Tuxan orders Maxwell's release under close surveillance for the purpose of attracting his allies, whoever or whatever they may be. He arranges for Maxwell to live in a State Reserve Hostel with a ration book to subsist on. In this setting, Maxwell meets three people who will interact with him: psychotherapist Dawna, retired gentleman Carl Mosley and resident Sydney Kitchen who remembers him from Glyderbank under another name. The narrative alternates between Maxwell's attempt to regain his memory and Tuxan's agents who are shadowing him. During the course of his quest, Maxwell encounters some persons who claim to have known him in the past as well as other persons who want him dead. Meanwhile, Dawna falls in love with him, even though she believes that he may be an alien from another planet. Maxwell's search for the truth results in his abduction, two killings and a startling revelation at Glyderbank regarding regenerative surgery.

The film version of *The Alien* has a different title, *The Groundstar Conspiracy*, but retains the inventive plot of the novel, including the climactic revelation. However, the deftly constructed script by Matthew Howard, a pseudonym for

Groundstar, the government's space research facility, is destroyed by a series of explosions.

Douglas Heyes, changes virtually everything else. The setting is not the future in Britain but the United States in the year of the film's release, 1972. Tuxan assumes a far more prominent role instead of a distant manipulator. The UFO storyline is eliminated along with the amnesiac's belief that he may be an extraterrestrial. (In the novel, the farmer confesses that he fabricated the UFO landing to attract tourists.) The amnesiac's name is Welles, not Maxwell, and he has a different history. The script combines the two women from the novel, Kaylee and Dawna, into the character of Nicole Devon, who also has a different history. Other changes will be apparent from the summary of the film.

The Groundstar Conspiracy begins with a series of explosions at Groundstar, a top-secret government space research facility. Six employees die and one man survives, though just barely. His face is burned beyond recognition but he is able to make his way to a nearby cottage in which Nicole Devon is temporarily staying. After he collapses at her door, she calls the police. A security card found attached to the injured man's clothing identifies him as John Welles, a computer technician at Groundstar. Classified material in his possession indicates that he caused the explosion to conceal the theft of secret documents for which the nation's enemies would pay enormous amounts of money. Further investigation reveals forged credentials and a fabricated identity. At the compound hospital, as doctors attempt to save the man's life, they determine that he will require extensive plastic surgery to repair his scorched features.

Tuxan (in the film, he is known only by his surname) is Groundstar's chief security officer and his sole objective is to find out who is responsible for theft, sabotage and murder. He has a brusque attitude and considers all persons connected to the project to be possible suspects. Tuxan intends to force the man called John Welles to reveal the name of the mastermind behind the crimes. Though Welles emerges from the hospital with his face totally bandaged, Tuxan badgers him for information. When the bandages are taken off, Welles stares at his scarred face without recognition. He claims to have amnesia and reacts with shock at the accusation that he killed six people. Tuscan tells him that he doesn't believe that his amnesia is genuine and proceeds to use brutal methods, including brainwashing and water-immersion, to discover the truth. The procedures have no effect on Welles whose few memories are of a woman on a beach near a Greek monument. Tuxan, finding his methods fruitless, tells Welles that he is sending him to a secret prison where he can rot until he tells the truth.

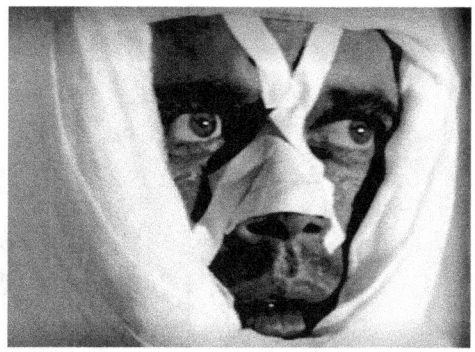

The suspected saboteur's scorched face required extensive plastic surgery.

An accident on the way to the prison allows Welles to escape. His only hope is to discover his past and hopefully prove his innocence. Although Nicole tells Tuxan that she never saw Welles prior to his appearance at her door, he believes that she may be the person to whom Welles was bringing the stolen data. Nicole is at a particularly vulnerable stage of her life due to a bitter

Tuxan infuriates Frank Gorsage (Tim O'Connor) and General Hackett (Alan Oppenheimer) by denying them access to the crime scene.

Science Fiction Thrills...Horror Chills

Nicole (Christine Belford) and Welles mistakenly believe that they are enjoying pleasurable moments away from Tuxan.

divorce and the loss of her parents. Frightened by Tuxan's incessant harassment, she is relieved when he finally releases her from custody, unaware that he has already bugged her home. Hoping to put the ordeal behind her, she returns to her apartment in the city. But her relief is only temporary as Welles invades her home to learn if he knew her in his past life. They are attracted to one another, not only because they are both recovering from trauma but also because they both despise Tuxan. Like other scenes in which Tuxan does not appear, his character still influences the progress of the story.

Tuxan's overbearing manner also alienates the officials in charge of Groundstar. These include Senator Stanton in whose state the facility is located, military director General Hackett and civilian director Frank Gossage, all of whom resent his arrogance, but he has full authority over them. They feel

Tuxan communicates with Welles who is inside the Groundstar office building; an unidentified actor plays the MP.

some satisfaction when they hear that Welles has escaped, proving that Tuxan is not as proficient as he thought. They don't realize that Tuxan planned the escape and is using Welles as bait to catch his accomplices. Not everyone dislikes Tuxan. His closest associate Bender and other subordinates meticulously follow all of his orders. Carl Mosley, the Groundstar publicist, appreciates the fact that Tuxan will keep him apprised of developments in the investigation. Groundstar's psychiatrist, Dr. Plover, also trusts Tuxan's judgment and has agreed in the past to administer his radical procedures upon suspects.

Since Tuxan has no respect for privacy, he closely monitors the activities of Nicole and Welles, even their most intimate moments. But Tuxan is not infallible and he is unable to prevent the kidnapping of Welles. In order to retrieve Welles, Tuxan must elicit information from Nicole and tells her that she and Welles have been under constant observation, even in her bedroom. This revelation drives Nicole into hysterics, but he pitilessly explains that loyal citizens must surrender their privacy for national security. After Welles escapes from his captors, Tuxan's team is able to locate the kidnappers, one of whom is Carl Mosley. A gun battle leads to the death of Mosley's associate, Charlie Kitchen, but Mosley survives. And Tuxan knows that his harsh methods will persuade Mosley to disclose the identity of the chief saboteur, who is exposed as Senator Stanton.

Welles knocks Carl Mosley (Cliff Potts) unconscious.

However, Welles must still uncover the mystery of his past. This quest brings him back to Groundstar with Tuxan on his trail. Welles breaks into Dr. Plover's office and is stunned to learn that Tuxan is responsible for his dilemma. When he furiously confronts Tuxan, the security expert calmly explains to Welles that doctors couldn't save the real Welles who died in the hospital. Tuxan needed a live Welles to expose his handlers and he found a volunteer named Peter Bellamy who, due to a personal tragedy, agreed to let Tuxan erase his memory and surgically alter his appearance. Knowing now that he is not Welles, Bellamy is relieved to learn that he is not a murderer, but he verbally and physically unleashes his fury upon Tuxan. But Tuxan remains unruffled. He is satisfied that he has solved the crime and has no regrets about the methods that he used to achieve his victory.

The Groundstar Conspiracy boasts assured direction by Lamont Johnson. The realistic characters and natural dialogue in Matthew Howard's screenplay help to make the proceedings believable, despite some far-fetched twists and turns. In the beginning of the film, Johnson depicts the contrast between the serenity that Nicole is seeking with the turmoil that quickly envelops her life. Similarly, the careful attention that he provides for the progress of her relationship with Welles is balanced by the swift pace of the action scenes which are

Welles physically forces Nicole to listen to him.

brief and brutal. In a similar vein, he emphasizes restraint in the torture scenes and doesn't exploit the grisly activities. He also has an appreciable eye for the beautiful shorelines of Vancouver, British Columbia which substitute for the U.S. Pacific coast. Johnson only directed about a dozen theatrical movies throughout his 45-year career and worked mostly in television, for which he received several Emmy and DGA (Directors Guild of America) nominations and awards. But this film, along with 1970's *The MacKenzie Break*, clearly shows that he excelled in both arenas, especially when he worked with gifted actors.

George Peppard provides a dynamic performance as Tuxan. His portrayal is particularly impressive because he doesn't attempt to make his character likeable. There is no hint of suppressed softness beneath Tuxan's pitiless surface. Peppard doesn't allow Tuxan to display any sympathy for the amnesiac, which makes his character especially loathsome in view of the climactic revelation that he knew all along that the man was incapable of remembering anything. And yet he was perfectly willing to torture him to convince the actual suspects that the real Welles was still alive. At the finale, he still doesn't expose any warmth toward Peter Bellamy, despite the fact that it was Bellamy's voluntary participation in the ploy that uncovered the traitors. And Tuxan even lectures Bellamy on how grateful he should be for now having the opportunity to start a new life. Then he simply turns his back on his speechless victim and walks away, calmly informing his subordinates that the danger is over. Tuxan is immoral and despicable. He has

George Peppard as Tuxan displays no regard for human decency.

Science Fiction Thrills...Horror Chills

Above an Italian poster featuring Peppard: opposite page a Japanese poster featuring Sarrazin

no regard for human decency and doesn't have a shred of conscience. But he is the film's hero. And it is Peppard's audacious performance that makes the character so charismatic, despite his pragmatic nastiness.

In the role of John Welles/Peter Bellamy, Michael Sarrazin flawlessly expresses his character's internal anguish and elicits the sympathy that is essential

to offset Tuxan's aloofness. He conveys emotional anguish, initially due to the mistreatment that he receives and then because of his despair at the thought that he may be a traitor and a murderer. Christine Belford is equally effective as Nicole Devon, particularly in the crucial scene in which she realizes that Tuxan has been monitoring her bedroom. The romance between Welles and

Nicole achieves credibility because of the sincerity with which both Sarrazin and Belford invest their characterizations. Welles' confusion and desperation combined with Nicole's emotional fragility appear quite genuine and renders their passion plausible instead of clichéd.

The Groundstar Conspiracy shows that the type of government manipulator represented by *The Mind Benders* has, a decade later, become institutionalized—and with more advanced means of torture. Like that earlier film, *The Groundstar Conspiracy* depicts some problematic issues that are no longer as fictitious as they were when the movie was initially released. It

Tuxan ascends the stairway to Groundstar's office building.

demonstrates how a government investigator can demolish an innocent man's identity and then use and abuse him to achieve his agency's goals. In 1974, *Who?* raised similar issues of identity. This movie illustrates how still another government investigator will deprive a person of his identity, on this occasion because he has suffered a terrible deformity and no longer looks human. The

investigator will brutalize the deformed person as much as the enemy government has abused him, though psychologically more than physically. But in this movie, the victim is not able to triumph over his ordeal.

The basis of *Who?* is the 1958 novel of the same title by Algis Budrys (1931-2008), an East Prussian-born American author of science fiction novels. (Budrys revised and updated the novel in 1975.) The setting is Europe in 1988, thirty years in the future. Two super-states, the Allied Nations Government and the Soviet Socialist Sphere, are engaged in a continual war of espionage. Shawn Rogers, ANG Security Chief, is on the Soviet-Allied border to meet with Russian officials who are returning Dr. Lucas Martino, an Allied physicist who was injured in an explosion. But Rogers is shocked to see that portions of Martino's body are now comprised of artificial components, including a prosthetic arm and a metallic-encased head and face. Soviet spymaster, Anastas Azarin claims that such extreme medical procedures were necessary to save Martino's life. But Rogers suspects that Azarin may have substituted a Soviet spy and that the real Martino is still a prisoner of the Russians who are draining his brain of classified information. The half-human/half-robot (the term 'cyborg,' short for cybernetic organism, was not devised until two years after the novel's initial publication) claims to be Martino but also admits to amnesia regarding the events surrounding the explosion. Since Martino was working on a top-secret project known as K-88, Rogers refuses to grant him a security clearance and keeps him under close surveillance to see if Soviet agents try to contact him. Consequently, the metallic man becomes depressed not only because Rogers prevents him from working on K-88 but because he is unable to prove his identity. Meanwhile, Rogers and Azarin increase the intensity of their psychological duel, each man trying to outwit the other. The novel builds to a melancholy conclusion which answers the question concerning the identity of the metallic man. At least, it provides an answer for the reader, though not for Rogers.

The film version of *Who?* is more faithful to the novel than the film version of *The Alien*. However, John Gould's literate screenplay does incorporate some changes. Like the earlier film, this film's setting is not the future but the year of the film's release, 1974, though the locations of Germany and Miami remain the same. The world is not divided into two super-states but the United States and the Soviet Union are still engaged in the Cold War. While the novel unfolds from Martino's perspective, the film progresses primarily from the viewpoint of Sean (different spelling) Rogers. The novel provides extensive details on Martino's history, specifically regarding his childhood and college years, which the author describes in chapters that alternate with the main narrative. The film tells the story in a more linear fashion, though flashbacks provide some important incidents in Martino's personal history, most significantly his relationships with Edith Hayes and Frank Haywood, as well as his treatment in Soviet captivity. Screenwriter Gould is successful in communicating some of Budrys' philosophical concepts, not an easy task in view of the limitations inherent within a film in comparison with the unlimited boundaries of a novel. Budrys' pessimistic comments on human nature, as evident from the fate of Lucas Martino, emerge intact on the screen. Regarding this fate, however, the film contains a more effective denouement. In the novel, after Rogers exits the narrative, the author provides a lengthy flashback to the Soviet Sphere that explains the mystery of the metallic man's identity. The film's conclusion is more suspenseful since it crosscuts between Rogers' final meeting with the metallic man and Azarin's attempts to substitute an imposter for the scientist.

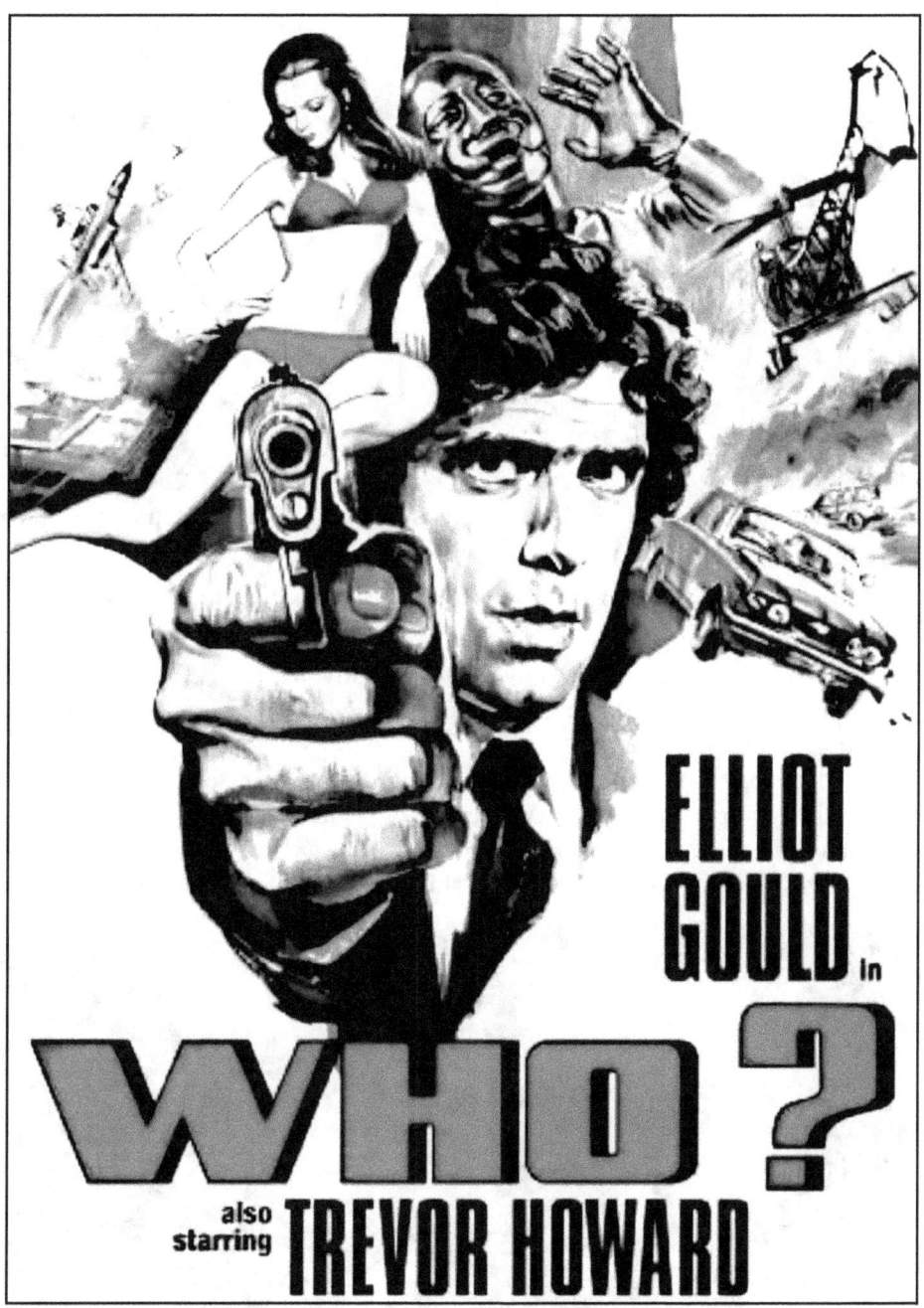

Who? begins at Checkpoint Charlie, the borderline between East and West Berlin, as American agents await the return by communist officials of American scientist Dr. Lucas Martino after six months in their care. Martino, who had been in charge of a top secret government defense assignment in Florida called the Neptune Project, was in Germany for a conference when he was in

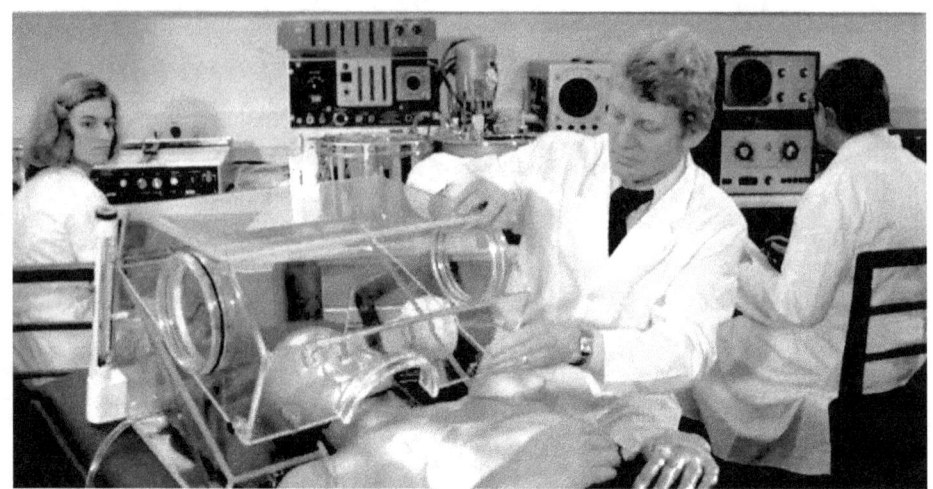

East German medical staff have encased most of Dr. Lucas Martino's (Joseph Bova) face in metal.

an automobile accident and, according to Communist authorities, was horribly disfigured. Consequently, doctors could only save his life by implanting metallic devices and artificial organs into his body; in addition to one metallic arm, his entire face and head are now encased in metal with only his eyes and mouth appearing human.

FBI agent Sean Rogers has to determine if the person that the Soviet Union has returned is actually Martino. Rogers knows that the man with the metallic face, whom he calls 'metal-man,' could very well be the real Martino who wants to return to work and serve his country. But the agent is aware that

Colonel Azarin (Trevor Howard) is responsible for Martino's (Joseph Bova) existence as half-man/half-robot.

Sean Rogers (Elliott Gould) suspects that Martino could have been brainwashed or could be an imposter.

his nemesis, Colonel Azarin, could have brainwashed Martino into becoming a traitor or could have substituted an imposter to gain access to highly secret data. Because of his suspicions, Rogers cannot allow the metal-man to resume his management of Neptune. Instead, though colleagues Finchley and Haller are inclined to believe the man behind the mask, Rogers subjects the metal-man to a grueling interrogation to discover the truth. When this interrogation proves fruitless, he transports the metal-man back to his home state of Florida and releases him from custody. But he keeps him under close surveillance to determine his real identity.

KGB spymaster Colonel Azarin is an equally obstinate agent who instigated the accident to abduct Martino. But the plan went awry and the scientist was almost fatally injured, leading to the radical surgery. Unknown to the Americans, if Azarin had allowed Martino to convalesce at a medically approved pace, the patient could have been restored to relative normalcy with extensive plastic surgery. But the spymaster demanded that the East German surgeon make the patient available for interrogation as soon as possible, thus dooming him to life as half-human/half-robot. Flashbacks of the Russian agent's unremitting interrogation of his prisoner in the past are intercut with his American counterpart's equally brutal questioning of the metal-man in the present. Following unsuccessful attempts to obtain information about Neptune, Azarin utilizes brainwashing to try to convert Martino into a double agent. If such methods fail, Azarin intends to persuade former Neptune scientist and defector, Frank Heywood, to assume Martino's identity under the guise of another metallic transplant.

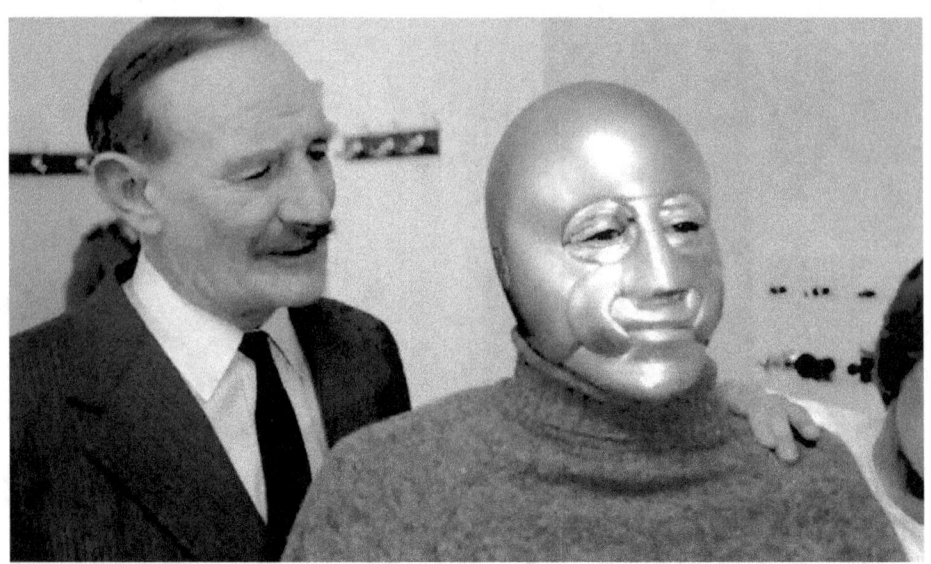

Azarin's insincere concern for Martino conceals his ruthlessness.

Caught in the crossfire between Rogers and Azarin is the man who claims to be Lucas Martino. The metal-man realizes that his physical appearance arouses various emotions from people, ranging from curiosity to horror. Despite this, he expresses loyalty to his country and pleads for a chance to return to work on the Neptune Project. However, he quickly becomes aware that Rogers neither believes nor trusts him. He then hopes to prove his identity by meeting with people from his past. But his former colleague, Dr. Besser, is shocked at his appearance and is not certain of his identity. His closest friend, Frank Haywood, has reportedly died, his defection being unknown. He attempts to rekindle his relationship with Edith Hayes, the woman that loved him, but his reunion with her is distressing. He also learns that the family farm on which he was raised is in ruins since the deaths of his parents. His uncle and cousin, in whose restaurant he worked as an adolescent, have also died. Another former lover, Barbara, has disappeared. Consequently, the metal-man becomes increasingly depressed.

Rogers is conflicted about his task. He wants to believe the metal-man but yet he cannot overcome his reservations, due in part to his suspicious nature as well as his distrust of Azarin. Because of his fear of failure and despite increasing evidence that his subject is telling the truth, Rogers constantly finds reasons not to believe him. For instance, the fact that the metal-man visits Edith should be proof that the man is whom he claims to be, particularly in view of the intimate conversation that Rogers listens to after bugging Edith's apartment. But though such behavior indicates that he is the real Martino, Rogers believes that the metal-man may be shrewdly trying to convince his trackers that he is not an impostor. Similarly, when his colleagues argue in defense of Martino, Rogers

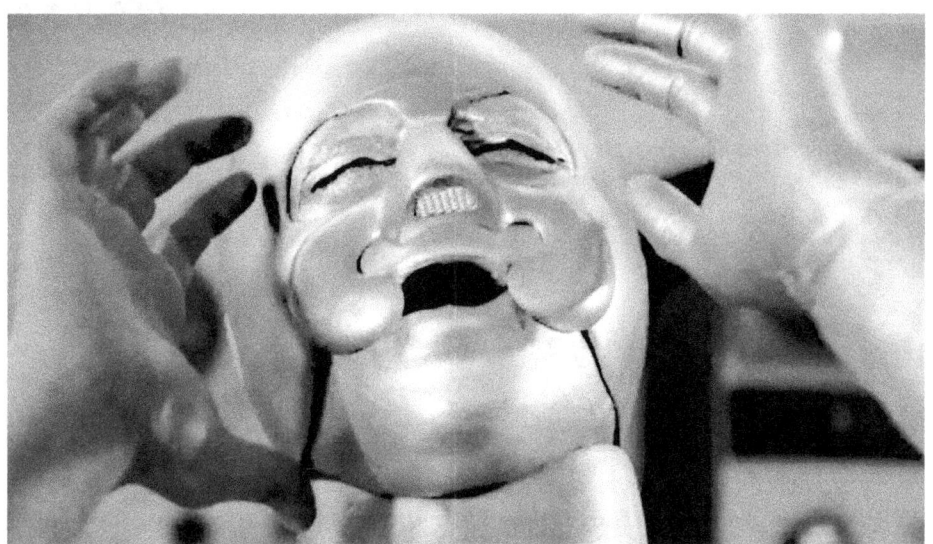

Martino reacts painfully to the endless Soviet interrogation.

has to increasingly rationalize his suspicions by submitting devious reasons for the suspect's actions. This internal impediment within Rogers is the primary reason that he will remain as frustrated as the man who claims to be Martino.

Ultimately, the man with the metallic face is indeed revealed (to viewers but not to Rogers) to be Lucas Martino. Flashbacks disclose that Azarin's frustration upon being unable to either indoctrinate Martino or substitute an imposter precedes his reluctant release of the man with the metallic face. Upon regaining his freedom, Martino is in an emotional state bordering on hysteria due to his horrific experiences as well as his bizarre appearance. But he hopes to resume some semblance of a normal life. He desperately needs acceptance and understanding from his colleagues along with compassion from his fellow citizens. But he encounters only suspicion and fear. He eventually loses the will to establish his identity. After enduring so much misery, all he wants to do is be alone on the family farm, his mind as broken as his body. The once-idealistic scientist who wanted to improve humanity now withdraws from human society.

The sequence with Edith is important to fully understanding Martino's acceptance of his fate. Martino's account of their past relationship reveals his responsibility for the emotional pain that he caused her. In the novel, Edith was divorced and had a daughter; it is partly the child's fearful reaction to Martino's appearance that compels him to leave the apartment. The film places more emphasis upon Martino's inherent faults. In effect, Martino viewed Edith as a problem that needed to be solved instead of a human being who loved him. Ironically, this is similar to Rogers' tendency to see Martino not as a person but as a puzzle to unravel. Thus, Martino and Rogers are, at least in their tendency to objectify people, mirror-images of one another. After Martino leaves,

Martino's reunion with Edith (Kay Thornburgh) is emotionally distressing for both of them.

Edith's last words to Rogers are heartrending, indicating her recognition that she will always be lonely, just as Martino will always be lonely. They will both live out the rest of their lives in solitude, sadly not too far from one another.

Rogers is doomed to a similarly sorrowful fate. Because of Martino's value to Neptune, Rogers' superior finally instructs him to allow the metal-man, whomever he may be, to return to work. But when Rogers visits Martino on his farm, he learns that this consent comes too late. Like Martino, Rogers also doesn't achieve his goal because he couldn't overcome his suspicions and because his vanity wouldn't allow him to admit his mistake. He thought that he could compute the concept of humanity along with such concepts as trust and patriotism, which he realizes too late are futile objectives. Thus, he dooms not only Martino to obscurity but himself to failure. In effect, because of his determination to outfox Azarin, he completes the destruction of Martino that Azarin initiated. More devastating, he causes the termination of the Neptune Project. At the end of the film, Rogers is a defeated man. When he finally addresses Martino by his first name, he admits to himself that he has been wrong all along. He has failed Martino, himself and his country.

Jack Gold's astute direction of *Who?* is perfectly in tune with John Gould's script. Gold directs the film in a realistic style, despite some fantastic trappings. Though there are a couple of action scenes, it is the dialogue and characters that propel the film. In this sense, the movie is a character study, not only of Martino but also of Rogers. Though the film's external theme is Rogers' quest to solve the mystery of the metal-man's identity, many scenes emphasize Martino's internal attempt to prove not only his identity but his humanity. The scenes of Martino trying to adjust to a normal life amidst the glares of onlookers are distressing because all of the people, like Rogers, cannot see beyond the

**Above: Azarin tries to trap Martino with questions about his family.
Below: Rogers also quiries Martino about his family.**

metallic face. Similarly, Gold presents the interrogation scenes in both American and Russian sectors in the same manner as other Cold War thrillers, which makes the more fantastic scenes credible. Interestingly, the director depicts all of Martino's personal flashbacks with the camera functioning as the scientist; thus, Martino's screen presence is limited to his metallic existence. The numerous flashbacks are never disruptive to the main narrative due primarily to the smooth transitions, with each flashback having a direct connection to the scenes that precede and follow them. Consequently, as the pieces of the puzzle gradually fit together, the film builds intriguingly to its surprising and sorrow-

Rogers tries to justify his suspicions about Martino to his colleagues.

ful climax. Similar to Lamont Johnston, Jack Gold spent most of his career in television, a medium in which he received many BAFTA nominations and awards. But *Who?*, along with *The Medusa Touch* (1978), demonstrates that his tremendous skill was not limited to the small screen.

Elliott Gould initially appears restrained though obstinate as Sean Rogers. Like *Groundstar*'s Tuxan, Rogers has the callous tenacity of a single-minded investigator and the self-possessed morality of a patriot who is devoted to serving his country. But, unlike Tuxan, it eventually becomes obvious that he has a conscience. The actor succeeds in suggesting, through moments of contemplation, that Rogers is struggling internally to justify his cruel treatment of the metal-man who, if he is genuine, has already experienced appalling pain. It is a difficult portrayal because Gould has to suppress his character's conflicting emotions until the climactic scene when he expresses his regret to the dejected man for his treatment of him. His expression clearly indicates his awareness that he is in part responsible for destroying the man's spirit. Gould's multifaceted performance succeeds in making Rogers fully three-dimensional and ultimately sympathetic.

Joseph Bova as Martino has the most demanding role, and he admirably succeeds in creating a pitiable character. It is quite a remarkable performance due to the limitations placed upon him. Since his face is encased in metal, he cannot convey his character's tortured emotions through facial expressions. Instead, he must suggest his anguish through his tone along with the use of his hands and arms. Through his occasional faltering speech, he manages to initially convey desperation tinged with hope. But as his professional and personal lives gradually dissipate, his listless movements and dispirited speech reflect

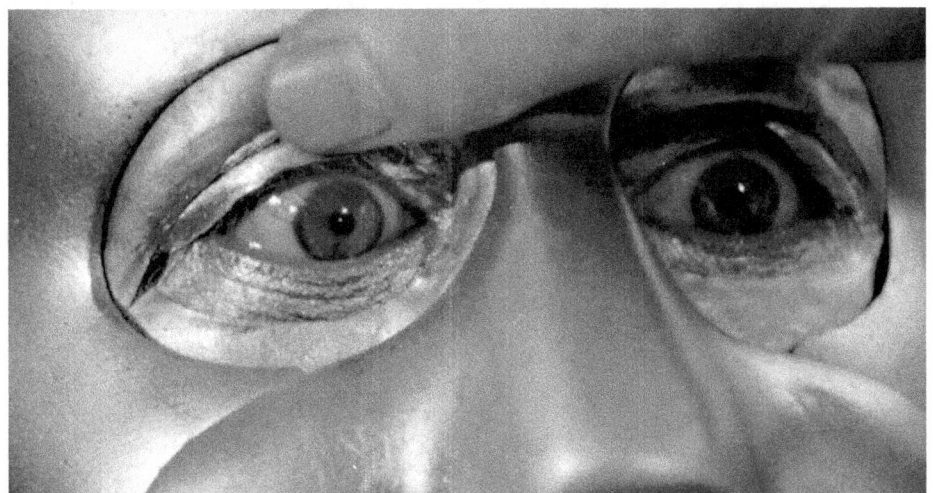

American doctors examine Martino's eyes to determine if they match the eyes of the man who once worked for the government .

his mounting despair and apathy. His increasingly lethargic manner clearly foretells his inevitable destruction by the forces of political bureaucracy. In effect, Bova skillfully communicates his character's descent from optimism into despair with heartrending sincerity.

Trevor Howard is effectively malicious as Azarin. With his credible Russian accent, he makes a suitable foil for Rogers and displays an equal amount of merciless resolve, though without his adversary's trace of morality. At the finale, the realization that all of his ploys against Martino have failed are obvious from the intense fury in his tone and expression. Though Kay Tornborg is in relatively few scenes, she is particularly memorable as Edith. Her extended reaction upon first seeing the man she obviously still loves encased within his metallic face is especially poignant. Her expression as she talks to Rogers on the phone is equally sad, especially in contrast with the happiness she projects in the flashbacks.

Unlike *The Groundstar Conspiracy*, *Who?* ends unhappily for each of the principal characters. While Tuxan emerges triumphant and unapologetic for his methods, Sean Rogers fails and regrets his methods. Peter Bellamy has the opportunity to find happiness with Nicole while Lucas Martino will never see Edith again. It is interesting that the rejuvenation theme has different consequences in both films. Mary Shelley in her classic novel *Frankenstein* provided her creation with the following agonizing words: "I am alone and miserable; man will not associate with me." Peter Bellamy has an advantage in that he has a new face and is able to find a mate with whom he can share his life, as evident from the final freeze frame showing Bellamy and Nicole frolicking on a beach. Lewis Martino, his face beyond repair, must endure the pain of rejection and

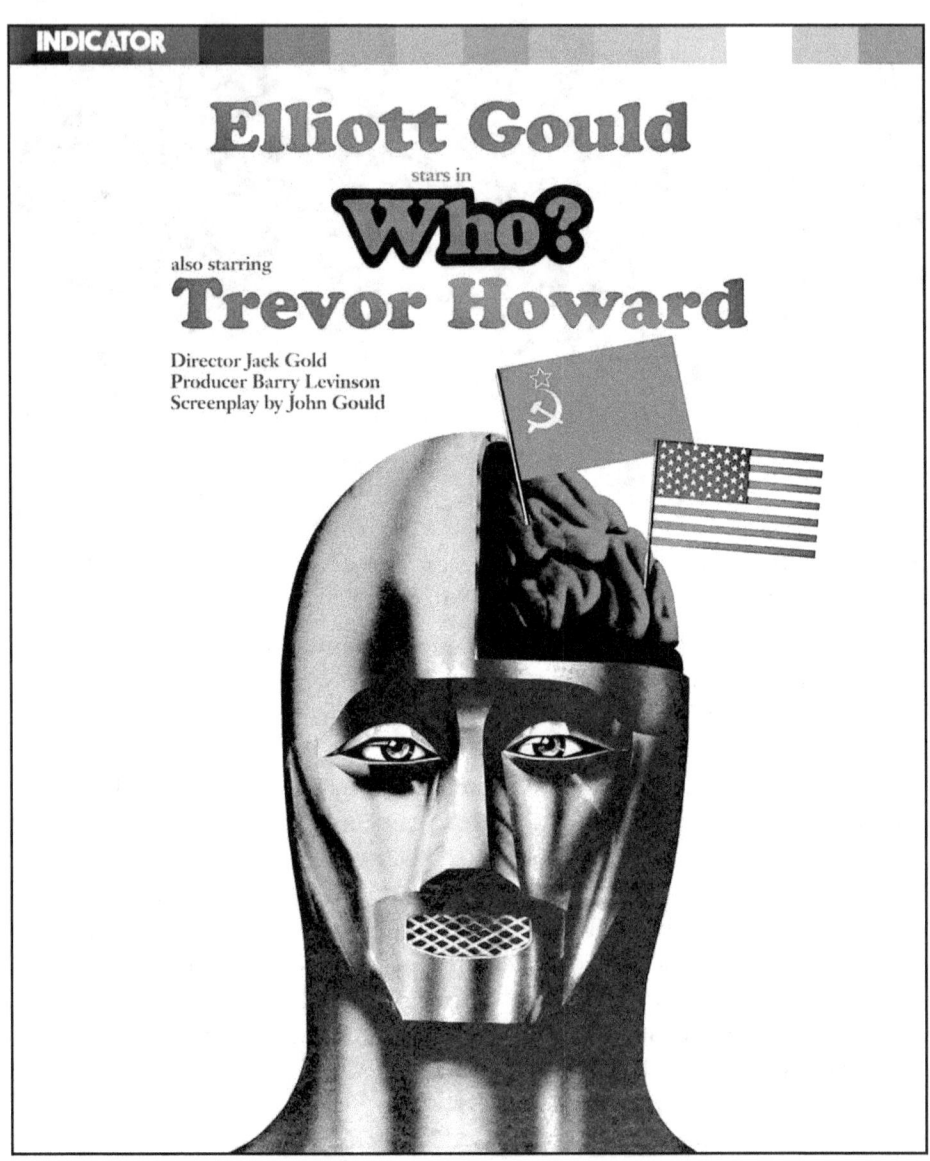

abnormality, as evident from the last scene that depicts him on a tractor, dooming him to ostracism and loneliness.

Both movies crashed at the box-office. *UMR* reports *The Groundstar Conspiracy*'s initial gross as less than $2 million while *Who?* didn't even clear the million mark. In his review of *The Groundstar Conspiracy* in *The New York Times*, Roger Greenspun wrote: "This is an espionage melodrama of skill and intelligence (and) is among the few genuine pleasures in recent movies;" he also makes a point of writing that it "opened rather modestly at neighborhood theaters." This indicates that Universal didn't have much faith in the movie, particularly since it subsequently played across the country without any fanfare.

Who? received even shoddier handling. Allied Artists acquired distribution of *Who?* in the United States but didn't release it until late 1975, almost eighteen months after British-Lion premiered it in England. AA reportedly tested it in a limited number of cities, but its poor performance precluded wider distribution. Admittedly, the movie could have had a more intriguing title. Then again, the eventual video title of *Robo Man* wasn't much better.

Reference books provide interesting assessments of the two movies. In *Science Fiction: The Film Encyclopedia* (William Morrow; 1974), Phil Hardy calls *The Groundstar Conspiracy* "a slick thriller variant on the Frankenstein theme with Sarrazin giving a carefully calculated performance as the monster and Peppard standing for the doctor." Hardy was less impressed with *Who?* and calls it "a modest offering," adding: "Gold directs as though unimpressed by his own script." Hardy mistakenly assumes that director Jack Gold and writer John Gould are the same person; they are not and are definitely two separate individuals. John Brosnan in *The Science Fiction Encyclopedia* (Doubleday; 1979) calls *Who?* "a disappointing film version of Budrys' interesting novel, adding: "It is ponderous and fails to develop the fascinating possibilities offered by the novel." It is interesting how some movies can affect different viewers in different ways. For some people—well, at least one—*Who?* is a provocative movie that lingers in the mind long after viewing it.

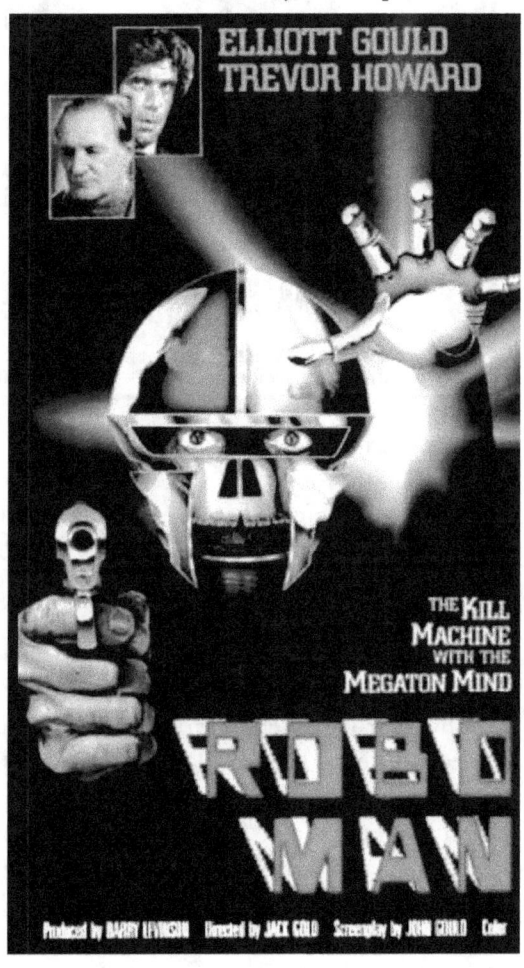

The Groundstar Conspiracy and *Who?* are primarily thrillers but they share underlying themes that depict societies in which advanced technology combined with political paranoia contaminate a democracy. The shared theme of the government's unchecked ability to spy on citizens and to monitor their intimate lives is all the more powerful for having been shown to be prophetic. Similarly, medical procedures that seemed fantastic decades ago are now quite plausible. Subjects such as bionic technology,

cyborgs and erasure of memories no longer belong to the realm of science fiction. The two films contain ideas that today remain challenging and provocative. They are also about people—human beings who suffer egregiously. The fact that they do this within a science fiction setting makes these two films distinctive and memorable within a genre that has regrettably become synonymous with computerized special effects.

The Groundstar Conspiracy
Credits: Executive Producers: Earl A. Glick, Hal Roach, Jr.; Producer: Trevor Wallace; Director: Lamont Johnson; Screenplay: Matthew Howard, based upon the novel by L. P. Davies; Cinematography: Michael Reed; Editor: Edward M. Abroms; Music: Paul Hoffert; Special Effects: Herbert Ewing

Cast: George Peppard (Tuxan); Michael Sarrazin (John Welles/Peter Bellamy); Christine Belford (Nicole Devon); Cliff Potts (Carl Mosley); James Olson (Senator Stanton); Tim O'Connor (Frank Gossage); James McEachin (Bender); Alan Oppenheimer (General Hackett); Roger Dresser (Charlie Kitchen); Ty Haller (Henshaw); Anna Hagan (Dr. Plover)

Who?
Credits: Producers: Barry Levinson, Kurt Berthold; Director: Jack Gold; Screenplay: John Gould, based upon the novel by Algis Budrys; Cinematography: Petrus R; Schloemp; Editor: Norman Wanstall; Music: John Cameron; Special Effects: Richard Richtsfeld; Art Direction: Peter Scharff

Cast: Elliott Gould (Sean Rogers); Trevor Howard (Colonel Azarin); Joseph Bova (Lucas Martino); Kay Thornburgh (Edith Hayes); Ed Grover (Finchley); John Lehne (Haller); John Stewart (Frank Heywood); James Noble (General Deptford); Lyndon Brook (Dr. Barrister); Michael Lombard (Dr. Besser); Joy Garrett (Barbara)

Capricorn One

Colonel Charles Brubaker is racing frantically for his life down the deserted road in the Mojave Desert. He is exhausted from lack of food and water but strains for every ounce of strength as he tries to outrun the men who are intent on killing him. And then, as if out of nowhere, a crop-duster plane suddenly appears beside him. Two men are inside, a pilot and another man who gestures wildly for Brubaker to jump into the plane. Desperate to remain alive, he leaps onto the wing of the plane as it takes off into the air.

This is one of many exciting scenes from the 1978 movie, *Capricorn One*. Upon viewing it in a theater, audiences frequently erupt into a spontaneous burst of applause as the rickety biplane swerves upward into the air and away from the would-be-killers. But that sequence is only a prelude to an exciting aerial sequence involving the biplane and two Black Hawk helicopters that are intent on blowing the old relic to smithereens. The faceless pilots of the two copters have to kill Brubaker because he is getting closer and closer to civilization.

What strange chain of events have led to this military officer being hunted like an animal by agents of his own government? To explain, it's necessary to return to the beginning of the movie.

Astronauts Colonel Charles Brubaker, Lieutenant Colonel Peter Willis and Commander John Walker are on the verge of beginning an extraordinary voyage through space. As they board the spaceship named Capricorn One, they

Sam Waterston, James Brolin and O. J. Simpson pose for a publicity photo.

anticipate being the first human beings to set foot on Mars. However, just prior to the launch, the chief of the National Aeronautics and Space Administration (NASA), Dr. James Kelloway, orders their clandestine removal from the ship. As the now-unmanned spacecraft blasts off into space, a taciturn pilot flies the stunned astronauts to an abandoned air base. Dr. Kelloway then informs them that he had to order their removal because a faulty life-support system would have killed them. He then must convince them to take part in a deception by pretending that they are on Mars when they will in fact be on an enormous sound stage alongside a bogus spaceship and fake Martian scenery. He further explains that, when the empty spacecraft returns to earth, it has been programmed to land at an isolated location where the men will be reunited with the ship to continue the charade that they have been to Mars and back.

Kelloway explains that if he had cancelled the flight, Congress would prevent additional funding for the agency and the exploration of space would be halted perhaps for decades. When he attempts to convince the astronauts of the necessity of cooperating with the sham, they resist. It is only Kelloway's threat to the lives of their families that persuades them to cooperate. This threat from Kelloway is an indication of just how desperate he is to salvage the country's space program. But by referring to powerful and ruthless forces whose future depends upon the success of the mission, he implies that he is also potentially expendable. The men reluctantly decide that they have no choice but to cooperate.

Judy Drinkwater (Karen Black) is the only person who believes Robert Caulfield (Elliott Gould).

Enter Robert Caulfield, a reporter who begins to sense that there is something amiss when NASA console technician Elliott Whitter notices something strange about

the transmissions that are allegedly from Mars but appear to emanate from earth. Caulfield thinks that Whitter is a bit batty until he mysteriously disappears. Upon searching for Whitter, Caulfield discovers that someone has totally erased the technician's identity. Caulfield suspects that only a powerful organization with government connections could be responsible for such a feat and begins his investigation.

Kelloway's devious plot initially succeeds. The astronauts remain in the hangar for several weeks simulating phony explorations of the Martian landscape which are filmed and shown on television to the nation. Everything works perfectly until a disaster strikes the return flight. As the unmanned ship enters the earth's atmosphere, the heat shield fails and the ship vaporizes. Since the entire nation's population believes that the three astronauts were in the spacecraft, they naturally presume that the men have been killed. To reveal that they are still alive would expose the deception.

Brubaker, Willis and Walker realize that they are now liabilities. They escape from the hangar, hijack a plane which unluckily has limited fuel and, after crash-landing in the desert, begin the long journey in different directions to reach safety. But with Kelloway's agents on their trail, they appear to have little chance to succeed. At the same time, Caulfield continues his investigation. When assassins try to kill him, he knows that he is getting closer to solving the mystery. And when police arrest him on a bogus drug possession charge, he realizes that the enemy is intent on stopping him one way or another. Unfortunately, he receives no support from his editor, Walter Loughlin, who considers

Colonel Brubaker (James Brolin) recoils in fear from a rattlesnake.

him a glory hound. Loughlin offers the beleaguered reporter neither sympathy nor assistance and eventually fires him. Only an ex-girlfriend, Judy Drinkwater, believes him and provides help.

The movie carefully builds momentum as the two interrelated stories converge. As the three astronauts separately struggle against overwhelming odds to contact another human being, Caulfield perseveres in his investigation. Because Kelloway comprehends the strategy of the astronauts, his agents apprehend Walker and then Willis despite the arduous ordeal that they have both endured. That leaves only Brubaker. The suspense steadily escalates through a series of increasingly thrilling sequences, not the least of which is the aforementioned rescue of Brubaker by Caulfield and an eccentric pilot named Albain. Yes, it is Caulfield in the biplane who reaches out to Brubaker. In the aerial dogfight that follows, it would seem that a dilapidated biplane would have no chance against high-tech choppers but don't count out

This archaic biplane will engage in aerial warfare with two high-tech government helicopters.

Caulfield desperately holds on to Brubaker to keep him from falling off the wing of the biplane.

Albain. He may be an oddball, but he is an expert pilot and no young whippersnapper military pilots are going to outmaneuver him. This leads to an exhilarating sequence with incredible aerial stunt work that ends in an explosive climax. The film then provides a catharsis with a highly emotional ending as Brubaker and Caulfield interrupt the ceremony in honor of the three supposedly deceased astronauts.

Capricorn One is often categorized as a conspiracy thriller because it depicts NASA officials fabricating a phony space mission. Some critics of the film ridicule it for feeding into the belief of skeptics that the 1969 moon landing was a hoax. But the film clearly states that NASA has already achieved a monumental success by landing on the moon. The flight to Mars is the next step in humanity's conquest of space and would be justification for the continued existence of the agency, which has gradually lost the support of the public due to apathy as well as disgust with national scandals. It is vital that the flight to Mars succeeds not only to restore the public's pride in their country but to establish the nation's supremacy in the midst of the Cold War. Among the rather sparse crowd of spectators watching the historic launch is Congressman Hollis Peaker but it is significant that the Vice President is in attendance and not the President, an indication of the lack of interest from the White House.

Capricorn One received many unfavorable reviews. Vincent Canby in *The New York Times* called the movie "humorless comic-strip stuff (and) a stylistically bankrupt melodrama." Many critics pointed out the implausibility of maintaining such a deception for an extended period of time. But these critics miss the point. There are obviously scientific plot holes and contrivances in the script. But this is not a serious exploration of government conspiracies such as, for instance, Alan Pakula's superb *The Parallax View* (1974). This movie utilizes the conspiracy as a set-up for what is essentially an action/adventure movie. Audiences leaving theaters didn't question the legitimacy of the moon landing but instead were delighted to be entertained. And they were already aware of government officials lying to them since this movie was released after the political assassinations of the Sixties, the Vietnam War, Watergate and the exposure of the illegal activities of intelligence agencies. In fact, the movie references both Watergate and the JFK assassination. This movie was designed to be escapist entertainment, a diversion from the sordidness of the real world. The movie contains good guys and bad guys, heroes and villains.

One of the astronauts faces the television camera during the fake telecast.

Brubaker, Willis and Walker are three genuine heroes, three husbands and fathers who would probably be willing to sacrifice their lives for their country under necessary circumstances. They have always been aware of the dangers

James Brolin, O. J. Simpson and Sam Waterston in another publicity photo.

Brubaker prepares to pummel one of Kelloway's agents.

of space travel and the innumerable disastrous crises that could occur at any time on their voyage through space. But yet they still risk their lives to explore unknown territory and advance humankind. However, being murdered by their own agency is not part of the deal. They believe that they have the moral and legal right to oppose a merciless organization that views them not as human beings but as impediments to progress. In contrast, Kelloway honestly believes that they are being selfish for wanting to live.

Dr. Kelloway is not an inherently evil man. He concludes with some perverse logic that he must order the deaths of the three men or witness the termination of his agency's endeavor to conquer space. To Kelloway, nothing is more important than traveling to another planet, establishing a colony and eventually preparing for flights to other planets in the solar system. Kelloway decides that Brubaker, Willis and Walker are expendable and must sacrifice their lives for the good of the country and for the ultimate benefit of humanity. Their families will have the knowledge that they died as martyrs and will forever be enshrined as national heroes. Actually, this leads to a flaw of the movie, and it concerns the fates of Willis and Walker. Following their capture, were they killed, or will they eventually be reunited with their families like Brubaker? The movie doesn't answer this question.

So, is Kelloway a villain? Absolutely, but with a caveat. He commits some loathsome acts, but they are due to patriotism and not selfishness. He assesses the lives of three men compared to the advancement of civilization and the progress of the human race. To Kelloway, it seems like a small price to pay. But he suffers from the delusion of grandeur which often infects persons in positions of power. He has assumed the right to determine who lives and who dies. He rationalizes this by knowing that generals and commanders in war frequently have to make such decisions with far more than three lives at their disposal. And he sees himself in a war with ignorant bureaucrats and an indifferent public.

Peter Hyams directed and wrote the screenplay for *Capricorn One*. The script seamlessly combines action, thrills, suspense and intrigue with an occasional infusion of humor. The increasingly futile attempts of the astronauts to survive achieves intensifying pathos, especially in view of Kelloway's established efficiency. Hyams tells this story not only from the viewpoint of the three astronauts but also from Kelloway's perspective as he systematically charts the escape routes of his prey. Caulfield's investigation

seems equally futile in the face of an enemy that has tentacles reaching into every phase of the government. But his persistence pays off as he gradually discovers clues that lead to a solution to the mystery. The script also introduces a third plot involving Brubaker's wife who gradually assumes an important role as the story proceeds. The script is an excellent example of how to connect several plot threads into a cohesive narrative.

Hyams films the action sequences with energetic proficiency. The climactic biplane and chopper pursuit sequence in particular provides edge-of-the seat thrills. Incidentally, during the course of the chase, the director presents a haunting scene in which the two choppers turn and face one another as though communicating in aerial sign language. It is a moment that is absolutely chill-

Caulfield bargains with Albain (Telly Savalas) to search for Brubaker.

ing because the choppers seem like alien predators with minds of their own. There is also the exciting scene in which Caulfield tries desperately to regain control of his speeding car before he crashes to his death. But Hyams also adds a delicate touch to Caulfield's scenes with Kay Brubaker that illustrate the reporter's sensitivity as well as the love that the grieving Mrs. Brubaker has for the husband that she believes is dead. And the scenes between Caulfield and Judy contain a playful banter that provides just the right amount of mild but unobtrusive humor.

The cast is topnotch. Elliott Gould has often been accused of repeatedly playing the same kind of laid-back character, which is incorrect. Gould has credibly played a variety of roles from the conflicted investigator of *Who?* to the timid bank teller of *The Silent Partner*, from the tortured archaeologist of *The Touch* to the inept song-and-dance man of *Harry and Walter Go to New York*. Though Robert Caulfield is initially an easygoing, blasé character not unlike some of his other portrayals, it gradually becomes clear that he has become jaded by his inability to score a big scoop. Through variations

Judy and Caulfield interview Kay Brubaker following the lift-off.

in his expressions and demeanor, Gould suggests an awakening of Caulfield's conscience, as though he had settled into a self-pitying rut but now seems to remember why he became a journalist. He begins to realize that his continuing apathy plays into the hands of a duplicitous organization. The realization that government officials are manipulating the media and snuffing out human lives stimulates his long-suppressed integrity and converts him into a dogged investigative journalist. Gould conveys all of these qualities to create a distinctive portrayal of a self-centered loser who becomes an intrepid champion.

James Brolin as Brubaker, Sam Waterston as Willis and O. J. Simpson as Walker portray the three astronauts with notable conviction. Brolin has the advantage of portraying not only the leader of the group but a character whose wife has a prominent role. Thus, the script conveys not only Brubaker's heroic qualities but also the emotional pain that his wife is experiencing. During his escape, the scene with a rattlesnake is truly memorable not only because it por-

Brubaker runs for his life from Kelloway's agents; this photo appears to have been superimposed over a photo of the stationary biplane.

trays the depths to which this national hero has descended but because Brolin's expression of both disgust and desperation leap off the screen. It is a terrific performance. As Willis, Sam Waterston provides some comic relief with his witty responses, but it soon becomes clear that Willis uses his sense of humor to conceal his abject fear that he is going to be murdered. O. J. Simpson's portrayal of Walker is perhaps his most dramatic performance, and he is particularly convincing as he reaches the point of physical collapse. Both Waterston and Simpson shine in scenes just before their capture with each actor credibly displaying total despondency with heart-rending despair.

Hal Holbrook could have made Kelloway an unmitigated villain but instead he faultlessly suggests that his character despises what he has to do but sees no alternative. During his lengthy speech in which he attempts to justify the deception to the astronauts, Holbrook plausibly conveys desperation, exasperation and eventually an agonizing reluctance to articulate the sinister connotations behind his words. This speech alone reveals the actor's undeniable skill. After the escape, when Kelloway directs the hunt for the three astronauts, never once does Holbrook indicate any pleasure in what his character has to do. It is a complex portrayal because, though Kelloway commits monstrous acts, Holbrook transmits his character's belief that he genuinely believes that his motives are altruistic. His expression of shock and disbelief at the conclusion is unforgettable.

The impressive supporting cast contributes to the film's effectiveness. Brenda Vaccaro is affecting as Kay Brubaker; as one example of her comprehension of her character, her subtle expressions upon Kelloway's visit to her home furtively reveals her internal feelings. David Doyle as Walter Loughlin is quite

Dr. James Kelloway (Hal Holbrook) supervises the pursuit of the three astronauts

the contrary to the conventional encouraging editor depicted in many newspaper movies as he callously rebuffs Caulfield in his hour of need, though his movie clichés are amusing. Karen Black makes a guest appearance as Judy Drinkwater and is a fine sparring partner for Caulfield. Robert Walden as the mystified Whitter, David Huddleston as the politically-savvy Congressman Peaker and James Karen as the rather shallow Vice President Price all provide true-to-life portrayals. Lou Frizell has a brief but significant scene as an agency official who expresses immense pride and admiration for the astronauts; this character obviously represents official NASA, as opposed to his illicit colleagues. And special mention must be given to Telly Savalas who makes a guest appearance as the cantankerous but resourceful Albain, shamelessly chewing his scenes with amusing delight.

Also noteworthy is Jerry Goldsmith's pulsating score. The powerful title theme sets the stage with an 8-note motif that promises danger and suspense and is heard throughout the film. The theme is particularly notable in that it is effective without being bombastic. Unlike so many modern scores which raucously assault the senses, Goldsmith's theme reflexively stimulates emotions while seamlessly intertwining with the images on screen. The score also contains softer interludes, including a melancholy romantic theme for Brubaker and Kay as well as subdued themes for the three increasingly desperate astronauts as they attempt to reach safety. All of these themes converge—simultaneous with the convergence of the film's plot threads—with a rousing climactic celebration of Brubaker's apparent return to life.

This joyous ending may be one of the reasons that *Capricorn One* was successful at the box office. The three movies that Peter Hyams had previously directed, including *Busting* with Elliott Gould, had all been financial bombs and he had not directed a film in two years. But the public responded enthusiastically to his fourth movie. The *UMR* website reports its initial domestic gross (the movie premiered in Japan in late 1977 but didn't open in the U.S. or the U.K. until the following year) as $32 million which was terrific in view of its moderate cost.

Brubaker hides from Kelloway's agents who have landed their helicopters near the deserted service station.

Capricorn One may create feelings of paranoia in some people. But for most viewers, it is an entertaining movie that leaves viewers applauding at the finale as Brubaker and Caulfield race through the cemetery in slow-motion, triumphant smiles upon their faces as they both achieve their respective dreams. Brubaker is about to embrace his wife and children and Caulfield will most likely win the Pulitzer Prize for journalism. Take that, Mr. Loughlin.

Credits: Presenter: Sir Lew Grade; Producer: Paul N. Lazarus III; Director: Peter Hyams; Screenplay: Peter Hyams; Editor: James Mitchell; Cinematographer: Bill Butler; Music: Jerry Goldsmith; Production Design: Albert Brenner; Art Direction: David Haber; Special Effects: Bruce Mattox, Bob Spurlock, Henry Millar, Jr., Henry Millar, Sr.

Cast: Elliott Gould (Robert Caulfield); James Brolin (Colonel Charles Brubaker); Hal Holbrook (Dr. James Kelloway); Sam Waterston (Lieutenant Col. Peter Willis); O. J. Simpson (Commander John Walker); Brenda Vacarro (Kay Brubaker); Telly Savalas (Albain); Karen Black (Judy Drinkwater); David Huddleston (Congressman Hollis Peaker); David Doyle (Walter Loughlin); Robert Walden (Eliot Whitter); Lee Bryant (Sharon Willis); Denise Nicholas (Betty Walker); James Karen (Vice President Price); Lou Frizzell (Horace Gruning); James Sikking (Controller); Nancy Malone (Mrs. Peaker); Virginia Kaiser (Mrs. Price); Alan Fudge (Capsule Communicator).

The Medusa Touch

"The moment they kneel to pray, I will bring the whole edifice down on their unworthy heads!"

These words reveal the hatred that John Morlar feels for the establishment, for the government, for religion and, essentially, for humanity. Does this threat indicate the delusional mind of a lunatic? Or does it foretell death and destruction on a massive scale?

John Morlar is the central character in the 1978 motion picture, *The Medusa Touch*, starring Richard Burton, Lino Ventura and Lee Remick. It is about a man who believes that he possesses telekinetic powers. The movie fits into many categories. It begins as a crime film with traces of neo-noir; it develops into a suspenseful psychological thriller; then it enters the realm of supernatural horror before climactically evolving into a disaster film of epic proportions. Like *The Power*, this film concerns a man who has mental faculties beyond any other mortal. But unlike Jim Tanner of that earlier movie, John Morlar uses his powers to cause catastrophic events.

Although some reports indicate that the movie was successful in England and France, it was a box-office disaster in the United States. The *UMR* website reports that its total domestic gross was only $200,000. *The Fury*, which had opened one month prior to *The Medusa Touch*, grossed $27 million while *Carrie* grossed $33 million two years earlier. It is significant that both of these movies are about teenagers with telekinetic powers and are thus directly aimed at the teenage audience which, by the late Seventies, comprised an increasingly large percentage of the moviegoing public.

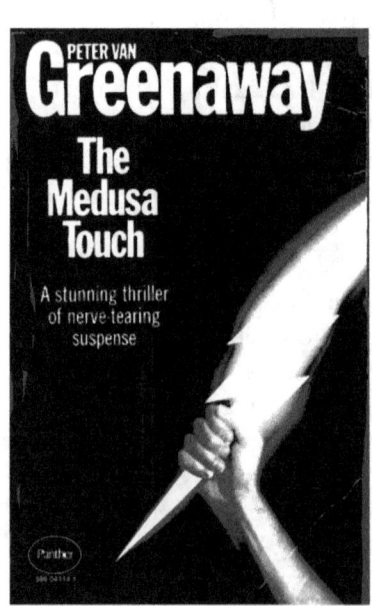

In contrast, *The Medusa Touch* is about adults and contains adult themes which may be why it played to empty theaters while those two inferior movies were huge hits. Negative reviews didn't help either. Vincent Canby in *The New York Times* wrote: "Morlar possesses telekinetic powers to make those of the characters in *The Fury* look frail; the movie is fuzzy on a number of key issues that possibly could have made it fun had they been sharper."

The Medusa Touch is based upon a 1973 novel of the same name by Peter Van Greenaway (1929-1988), a British author of thrillers with occasional science fiction or horror themes. As his work progressed, critics noticed an increasingly pessimistic view of humanity which

his fifth novel, *The Medusa Touch* reflects to some degree. John Briley, whose previous genre work was *Children of the Damned* (1963), adapted the novel into a screenplay that follows the novel fairly closely, with some exceptions. Most noticeably, he changes the sex of the psychiatrist from male to female and converts the novel's British detective, Inspector Cherry (the protagonist of several novels by Van Greenaway) into a French inspector who is assigned to Scotland Yard as part of an exchange program. The film omits many biographical details of Morlar's life that are included in the novel, such as his military service.

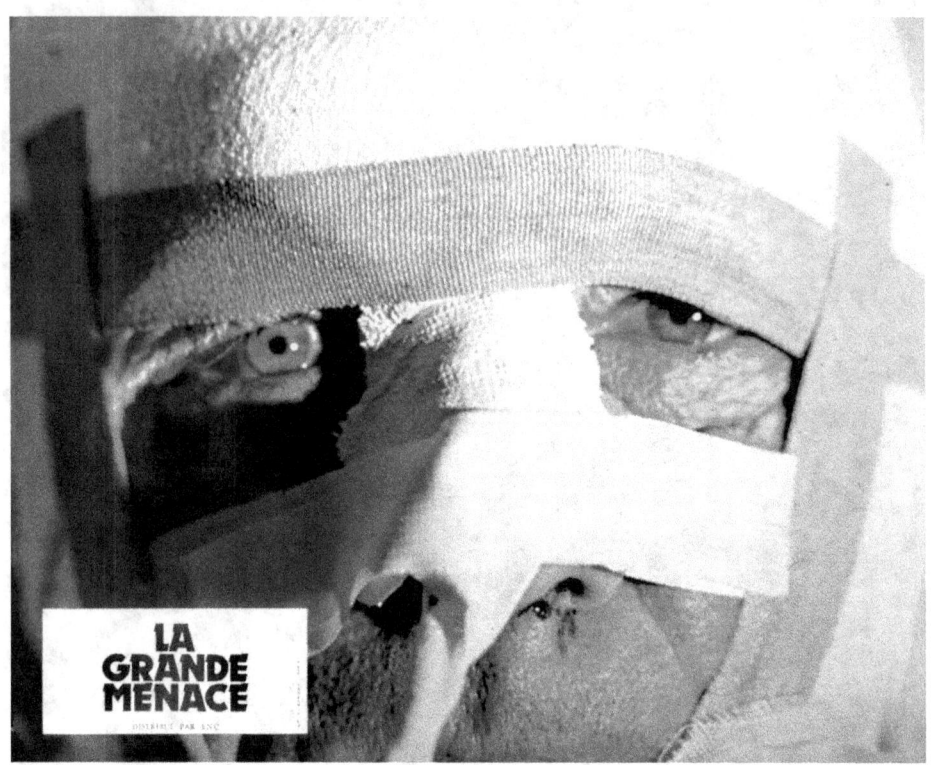

John Morlar (Richard Burton) has a smashed brain but refuses to die.

The film only hints at the political subtext regarding the reasons for the government's animosity toward Morlar, which the novel develops more extensively. And Briley does not identify the mysterious "L" that Morlar refers to in his journal, though the novel specifies his identity.

The Medusa Touch begins with the attempted murder of author John Morlar in his London flat by an unseen assailant who bludgeons Morlar's brains into mush as he watches a news report on television of a doomed American lunar landing. Inspector Brunel and his assistant Sergeant Duff assume, by the sight of the victim's brain tissue seeping out of his shattered skull, that he must be dead. But as they search for clues, Morlar suddenly starts breathing. An ambulance rushes him to a hospital where the medical staff quickly try to save his life. Meanwhile, Brunel continues his investigation to apprehend the assailant. Morlar's journal leads him to the victim's psychiatrist, Dr. Zonfeld, who informs him that Morlar believed that he had the telekinetic power to cause disasters by merely *willing* them to happen. Brunel considers this to be preposterous, which was Zonfeld's initial impression. However, as various people who knew Morlar provide facts about his life, it seems that a number of people who have harmed Morlar met with untimely deaths. As Brunel rides through London, there are signs of a more recent catastrophe involving a crashed Jumbo Jet airliner and a demolished skyscraper. There are also the reports of the impending tragedy aboard the lunar space mission. Brunel initially sees no connection between these events and his investigation. But his skepticism gradually crumbles as the comatose patient exhibits increasingly intense brain wave activity. Brunel eventually deduces that Morlar is plotting additional calamities. from a smashed brain that refuses to let his body die.

A superficial summary cannot provide the multifaceted intricacies of John Briley's script, the depth of the characterizations, the sharp dialogue or the philosophical and theological questions that the story raises. The script is a precise blueprint of intertwined themes. Each flashback provides new information about Morlar's relationships with other persons whose deaths he may or may not have caused. In turn, the scenes in the present reveal the increasing possibility of his connection to the recent tragedies along with implications of future catastrophes. The story develops from the perspective of the detective, a device that allows the viewer to see and experience only what he does and thus gradually come to believe the disturbing reality of the situation as he does. The result is a surprisingly plausible film, despite its implausible subject.

Jack Gold is the director and also co-produced the film with Academy Award winning editor (for *Lawrence of Arabia*) Anne V. Coates. Though he

Inspector Brunel (Lino Ventura) discovers that Dr. Zonfeld (Lee Remick) has committed suicide.

worked more frequently in television throughout his four-and-a-half-decade career, Gold also directed eleven theatrical films. Upon the release of his first movie, *The Bofors Gun* (1968), critics praised him as one of England's distinctive new talents. His fourth movie, *Who?* (1974, see previous chapter), revealed his versatility. *The Medusa Touch* was his eighth movie. His direction avoids sensationalism and creates the appropriate atmosphere to make the far-fetched events look credible. For each of the initial deaths, the director's staging of these scenes deliberately avoids assigning responsibility to the young Morlar and suggests an alternate explanation for the fatalities. Gold directs the investigation scenes in the manner of other police films while the relationship between the inspector and his subordinate implies a similar familiarity. Though the investigation assumes priority, Gold often displays reminders of the larger tragedies that have occurred in the surrounding environment, covertly linking the events. The meticulously detailed scenes of devastation in the streets add to the sense of authenticity which will make the cause of the tragedy when it is revealed seem equally believable. As the story progresses, reports of fatalities from the plane crash and the lunar mission along with potential hazards at the nuclear plant become increasingly prominent.

Brunel and Sergeant Duff (Michael Byrne) are shocked that Morlar is still breathing.

Gold and Briley provide a detailed exposition of the character of John Morlar that is chillingly credible, despite the unnatural circumstances that infuse his entire life. There is something very believable about Morlar and this is what makes the film so much more frightening than other films on the subject that appear more fantastic than real. Furthermore, the focus of this film is not on some trivial matter, such as who is taking whom to a high school prom, but about whether or not the human race deserves to survive. Beneath the surface of a horror story, the film raises questions about the nature of humanity. It provokes serious discussion about human beings and supreme beings, both good and evil. During the course of the story, it is suggested that Morlar may be either God's avenging angel or Satan's disciple of death. This sounds like profound subject matter and, indeed, simmering under the main storyline are very serious ideas to contemplate. A closer study of the movie will illuminate these ideas.

Richard Burton as John Morlar dominates the movie with a powerful performance.

The Medusa Touch introduces Morlar as an adult in a pre-credits sequence just prior to the murder attempt. In the film's first scene, the camera focuses on Edvard Munch's 1893 expressionistic painting *The Scream*, which is on the wall of Morlar's flat. It depicts a distorted person who is experiencing emotional suffering with mouth and eyes wide open in a screech of horror. Munch reported as inspiration for his painting the sight of blood red clouds caused by the setting sun accompanied by "an infinite scream piercing through nature." Critics have stated that the painting reflected the chaotic emotional state of the artist who had a lifelong fear of insanity. Morlar will also express his terror to his psychiatrist over going insane. From this painting, the camera moves slowly and settles upon Morlar who

The Scream by Edvard Munch

Science Fiction Thrills...Horror Chills

is intently watching the unfolding tragedy in space. He doesn't appear to be surprised at the sight of his visitor and makes a typically sarcastic remark as he discerns the visitor's deadly intent. He doesn't even try to evade the figurine of Napoleon as it repeatedly crashes into his skull.

The credits of the film then appear over Caravaggio's 1597 painting of Medusa, her hideous face caressed by serpents instead of hair. Anyone gazing upon Medusa's face, according to mythology, will turn to stone and die. During the course of the film, Morlar will furiously stare at certain persons who will die soon afterward. Brunel later explains to his subordinate, "Medusa is a monster who was created to do battle with the gods." As he grows older, Morlar will increasingly express his contempt for God and for those who believe in a deity. He will believe that, by destroying believers, he is engaging in a battle with God.

When Dr. Zonfeld describes to Brunel her experiences with Morlar, she explains her patient's beliefs as purely delusional. Her tone indicates disbelief as she relates to the detective Morlar's initial experience as a five-year-old child. In this flashback, young John cringes in terror as a malicious nanny fills his impressionable mind with fears of hellfire and damnation. The frightened boy silently and desperately pleads for help, not from God but from Lucifer. This is the first indication that he may be a child of Satan. Then again, he may only turn to the devil because of the images that the nanny placed in his mind. All that is certain is that a disturbed adult is frightening the daylights out of a vulnerable child. Suffice to say, something will happen that will prevent her from ever doing that again.

In another flashback that Zonfeld relates, John is 10 years old. At this time, he seems to be a normal boy, running and playing like any child of his age, hurrying to do his mother's bidding in an attempt to please her. But his parents, the two persons to whom he is closest, appear to consider him somewhat odd and he is obviously hurt upon overhearing their unkind words about him. Nevertheless, as he sits behind the wheel of his father's car, there are no signs to indicate that he wants to kill them. While he may have accidentally released the brakes of the automobile, it is also quite possible that his father did not secure the brakes.

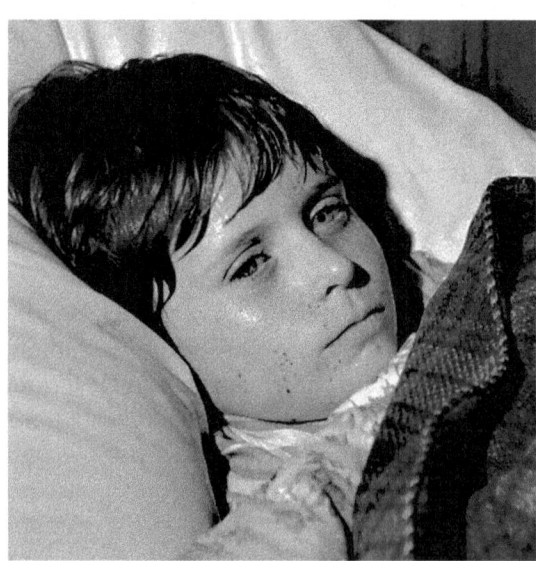

Adam Bridges as young John

Brunel believes that Zonfeld may be concealing information about Morlar.

Initially, Zonfeld appears to minimize the significance of these events to Brunel. But the detective discerns that the psychiatrist seems to be concealing information. In the next flashback, John is now a 14-year-old student in a boarding school, obviously wise beyond his years as he ignores a pompous schoolmaster. When John verbally embarrasses the teacher in front of the class, the teacher unjustly punishes him. (In the novel, the teacher is a pedophile, but this criminality is not in the film; however, when John reports to the teacher at nighttime, another boy is in the background, suggesting degeneracy.) This punishment will initiate a series of events that will end in an early demise for the teacher and for several students. Authorities determine the cause of the deaths to be accidental, which is quite possible in view of John's distressed emotional state caused by the teacher's cruelty.

Brunel also meets with a barrister, a former partner of the adult Morlar when he was practicing law. He relates a significant event that prompted Morlar to leave the profession. As a defense attorney, Morlar defended a young man, Loveless, who committed a minor act of defiance against the Imperial War Museum. From his spirited defense, it is apparent that Morlar has developed passionate anti-government and anti-war sentiments. He is extremely emotional about his beliefs but unwisely expresses them to Judge McKinley who takes his revenge upon the defendant. This will be the last case that the judge will ever hear. And one of the last things that the judge will see is Morlar's ominous stare, filled with anger.

This deadly gaze, similar to that of Medusa, tends to support the theory that the devil to whom the young Morlar prayed may have rewarded him with special powers. Two additional flashbacks hint at the possibility of Satanic influence. In a desperate effort to find an explanation for his powers, Morlar visits a fortune teller whose frightened response indicates that he detects an inherent evil within Morlar. And Mrs. Pennington, Morlar's former neighbor, makes the mistake of shouting too loud and pays the ultimate price, leaving her husband devastated. This same husband bitterly informs Brunel that he believes that Morlar is demonically possessed. However, at one point, Morlar emphatically denies possession, scornfully dismissing such a possibility as simplistic and superstitious.

It is also significant that Morlar's resentment of the government's militaristic policies is humane and negates the theory that he may be demonic. If he was satanic, he would applaud war. Instead, he vehemently expresses his anger against his government for sending thousands of young men to die in unnecessary wars and profiting from wholesale death and destruction. He condemns the establishment for its misuse of the atom to create a weapon of mass destruction. He will also criticize the American government for spending a fortune to send a spaceship to the moon while millions of people are starving.

Loveless does not again appear in the film—except possibly as a tramp. But there is that aforementioned "L" in Morlar's journal. In the novel, L is Lorimar,

Mrs. Pennington (Avril Elgar) will face the wrath of Morlar.

one of Morlar's former clients who provides him with information about the government's illicit activities. In the film, the Assistant Commissioner of Scotland Yard hints at this sub-plot when he informs Brunel that so-called interested parties want the case solved as quickly as possible. The novel depicts Loveless' imprisonment and eventual suicide. The film eliminates Loveless' death and L's identity remains unknown. Incidentally, the only other character in the film whose name begins with L is the recipient of the young John's prayer: Lucifer.

Brunel meets with Morlar's publisher who suggests that the reason for the government's hostility toward Morlar was the author's controversial novels (one of which is ominously titled *The Incinerator*) which may have contained politically sensitive information. But the intriguing part of this flashback occurs when Morlar, after looking out of the window, suddenly leaves the publisher's office to talk to a tramp who is sitting on a bench in a park. Morlar's concern for this nameless tramp, who is only seen from a distance, is apparent since he talks to him for several hours. If this tramp is Loveless, the fact that the government reduced his former client to poverty is the kind of injustice that would fuel Morlar's hatred toward the establishment.

Another incident in Morlar's past that Dr. Zonfeld relates to Brunel appears to have signified a turning point in his life. As Morlar returns home from work, he finds his wife, Patricia, in the company of her lover, Parrish. When Patricia tells John that she is leaving him and that he will never see her again, she doesn't realize how truthful her words are. This sequence demonstrates Morlar's embittered personality as he expresses both indifference and contempt toward his wife. But it also reveals his grief over the death of his child and his anguish over the child's deformed condition, about which Patricia makes a particularly nasty remark. The fact that Morlar was unable to sire a normal child suggests that perhaps his own birth may have been abnormal and that this is the source of his powers.

This incident definitely causes a change within Morlar. Prior to this event, Morlar did not think he had caused the deaths of the people who had harmed him. He only believed that he somehow sensed that those persons would die. But regarding his wife's death, he tells Zonfeld that he

Patricia Morlar (Marie-Christine Barrault) and Parrish (Jeremy Brett) are interrupted by Morlar as he returns home.

Science Fiction Thrills...Horror Chills

Morlar angrily tells Zonfeld about the birth of his deformed baby.

didn't just *know* that she was going to die. He now believes that he *made* her die but he doesn't know how. In Morlar's mind, this knowledge initiates severe anguish over the fact that he may have subconsciously also caused the deaths of his parents along with several schoolchildren. However, since he did not consciously instigate these deaths, he believes that some mysterious element is in place. He hopes that Zonfeld will give him the answer to this dilemma.

Morlar elicits sympathy when he agonizingly begs for help from the psychiatrist. After many sessions, Zonfeld still believes that he is mentally ill. She dismisses any kind of supernatural influence and believes that medication may be necessary to calm her patient's increased anxiety and depression. Her refusal to believe him pushes him over the edge and he succumbs to the seduction of his power. It is unfortunate for them both that she realizes only too late that she has been mistaken. When she witnesses his demonstration of his powers, she shockingly sees that he is not delusional. And for the first time, he is now causing the deaths of innocent people who have never harmed him. The horror of this appalling event convinces her that she must stop him from committing further acts of carnage. Sadly, she will fail. And when Brunel arrives at the same conclusion, he also will fail. Neither of them will be able to prevent the famous edifice from collapsing upon hundreds of worshipping people. But this horror is only a prelude to the nuclear devastation that Morlar is so obviously planning to inflict upon the entire world.

The Medusa Touch is quite provocative, particularly regarding the numerous religious references. During different stages of his life, Morlar's attitude toward religion fluctuates. From his diatribes, it is apparent that the human capacity for evil is one reason for his nihilistic beliefs. At one point he tells Zonfeld that he doesn't believe in either God or the devil. Yet, at another point, he bitterly states that he is "doing God's dirty work." He curses practitioners of organized religion for their hypocrisy and sarcastically sneers at the fact that "God and gentle Jesus are now the in-thing." Reacting to the many disasters all over the world, he states that "we are all the devil's children." And it is significant that a prominent cathedral filled with worshippers, whether their heads are unworthy or not, will eventually become the target of his destructive powers.

The film also succeeds as suspenseful and exciting entertainment. The script and direction proceed at a tempo which reflects the progress of the plot. The film begins at a methodical pace as Brunel gathers information from various sources that gradually dismantle his skepticism. As he begins to believe the reality of Morlar's powers, the pace of the film steadily increases. The tempo reaches fever pitch as he races against time to prevent a horrendous tragedy. In the final terrifying sequence of the film, Brunel and the doctor realize that the catastrophe unfolding before them at the cathedral, as terrible as it is, will actually seem insignificant compared to the nuclear cataclysm that neither they nor anyone else will be able to prevent.

Concerning the source of Morlar's powers, the film leaves this question unanswered. In fact, the film suggests some reason not known by science or the-

Bristol Cathedral was used as the location for the fictional London Minster Cathedral in the film.

ology, something beyond human knowledge. And this is what makes Morlar so frightening and yet so pathetic, for he may be as much a victim as a villain.

A complex character such as John Morlar required an actor of considerable skill to portray his many facets. Richard Burton had been a huge box-office draw in the 1960s but by 1978 he had not starred in a financial success for almost a decade. A string of flops throughout the 1970s (*Bluebeard*, *The Klansman*, *Exorcist II: The Heretic*, etc.) had considerably diminished his popularity. But when inspired, he could still prove that alcohol had not dissipated his innate skill. The previous year, he had delivered a fine performance in *Equus* (1977) but though that film was a critical success it was another financial disappointment. Following *The Medusa Touch*, he starred in two additional movies in 1978. He was excellent in *Absolution* (1978) but the movie continued his string of financial failures. His third release of the year was *The Wild Geese* which was hugely popular in most countries, though not in the United States due to poor distribution.

Burton has relatively few scenes in *The Medusa Touch* yet he dominates the film, not only because people talk about Morlar when he is not on screen but also because the actor infuses his character with such passionate intensity. He faultlessly conveys Morlar's misanthropy through his bitter tone and sour expression, aided at times by gritted teeth and bulging eyes. And yet he also imbues his character with pathos and suffering. He projects the mental anguish of a man who is expe-

Special effects shot being prepared for the plane crash scene.

riencing internal torment and is becoming increasingly unstable. The impact of Burton's precise elocution and perfect diction is also an enormous asset. He recites

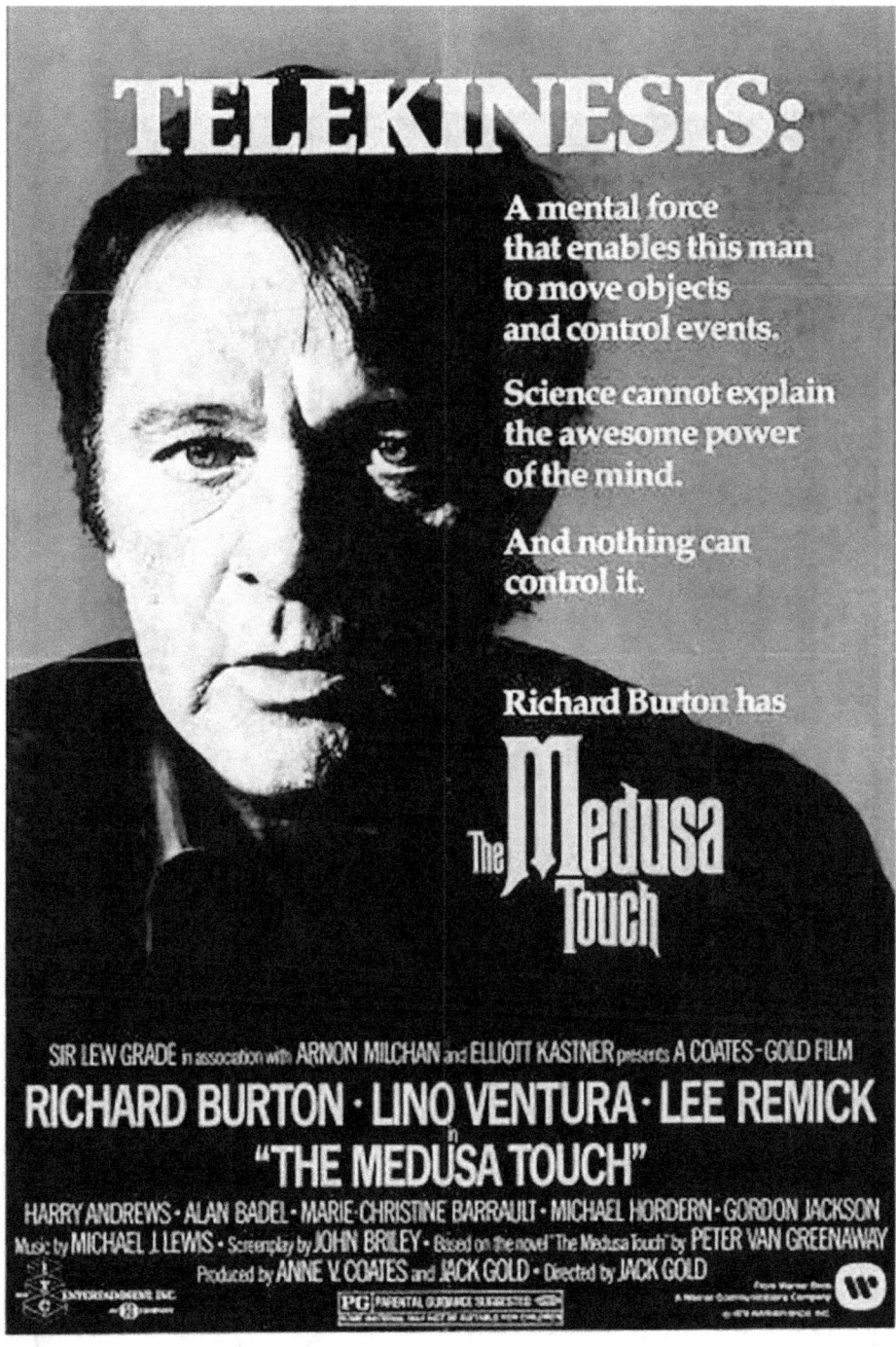

Italian poster for *The Medusa Touch*

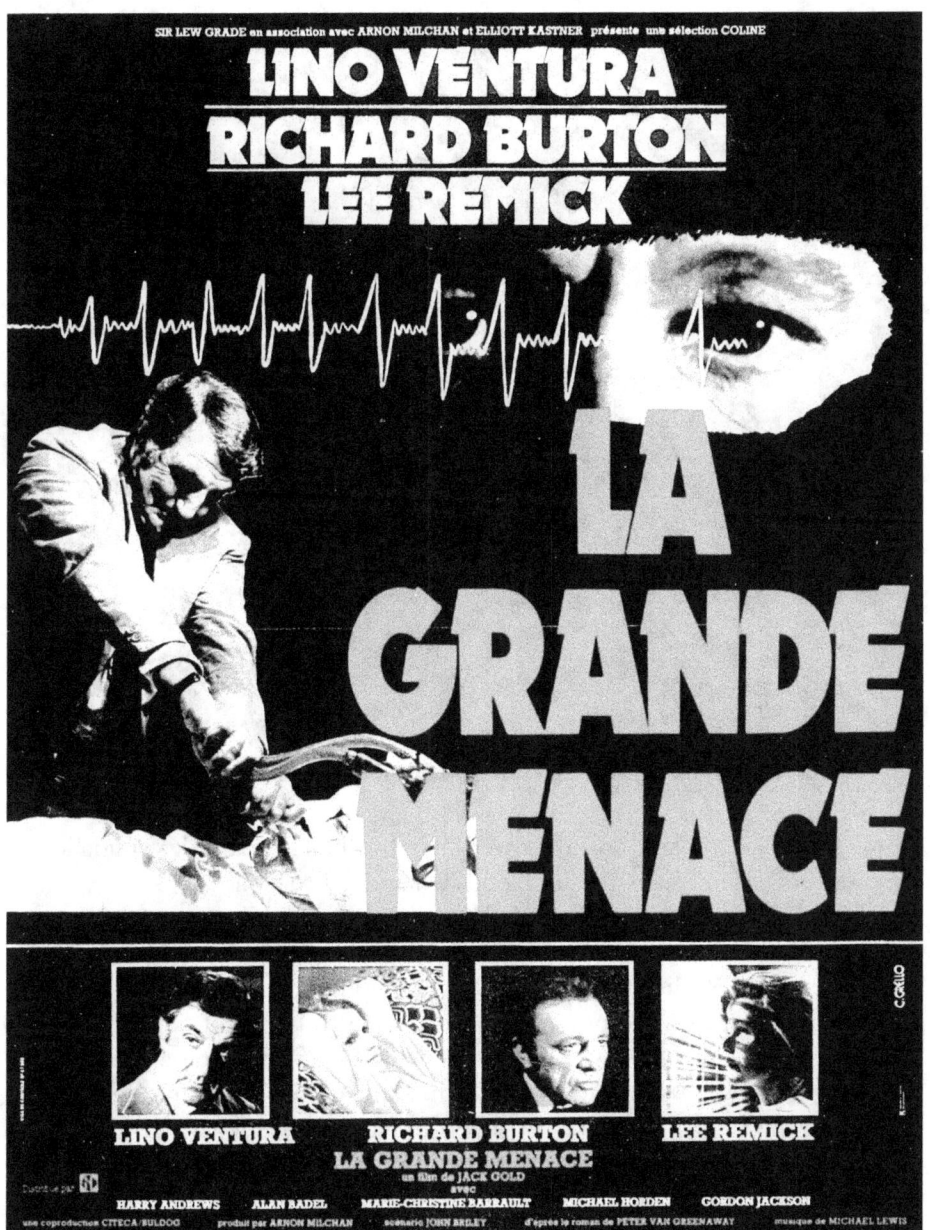

French poster for *The Medusa Touch*

his dialogue, particularly his passionate tirades against bureaucratic injustice, with every ounce of conviction. In the pivotal sequence with his wife, he hurls his acerbic insults toward her in such a pitiless manner that it almost evokes sympathy for her. And when he says to Zonfeld, "I have a gift for disaster," his words transmit total conviction. It is a masterful portrayal that convincingly reveals all degrees of Morlar's descent from desperation in his pleas for help, despondency over his con-

Morlar forces Zonfeld to watch him demonstrate his powers.

dition, fatalistic acceptance of his powers and, finally, a fanatical determination to use those powers to create massive bloodshed and destruction.

Lino Ventura was born in Italy but established his film career in France. Since the movie is an English-French co-production, his participation must have been part of the deal. Regardless, he convincingly conveys his character's evolution from skeptic to believer. Initially, he is not particularly expressive as he begins his investigation of what he assumes to be just another homicide case. The subtle differences in the manner in which he looks at Zonfeld as he slowly develops suspicion of her are particularly informative in view of later developments. As his pursuit of the truth steadily yields distressing information, he exhibits increased emotion along with a more vigorous speech and manner. The sequence in which he finally understands the meaning of "the West Front" is particularly effective. And in the final sequence, Ventura contributes immeasurably to the film's emotional involvement as he frantically attempts to terminate Morlar's increasingly powerful brain waves.

As Dr. Zonfeld, Lee Remick has a difficult role to play but she believably makes her character sympathetic and, ultimately, tragic. Upon her introduction, she must indicate that she is pretending to be surprised at her patient's

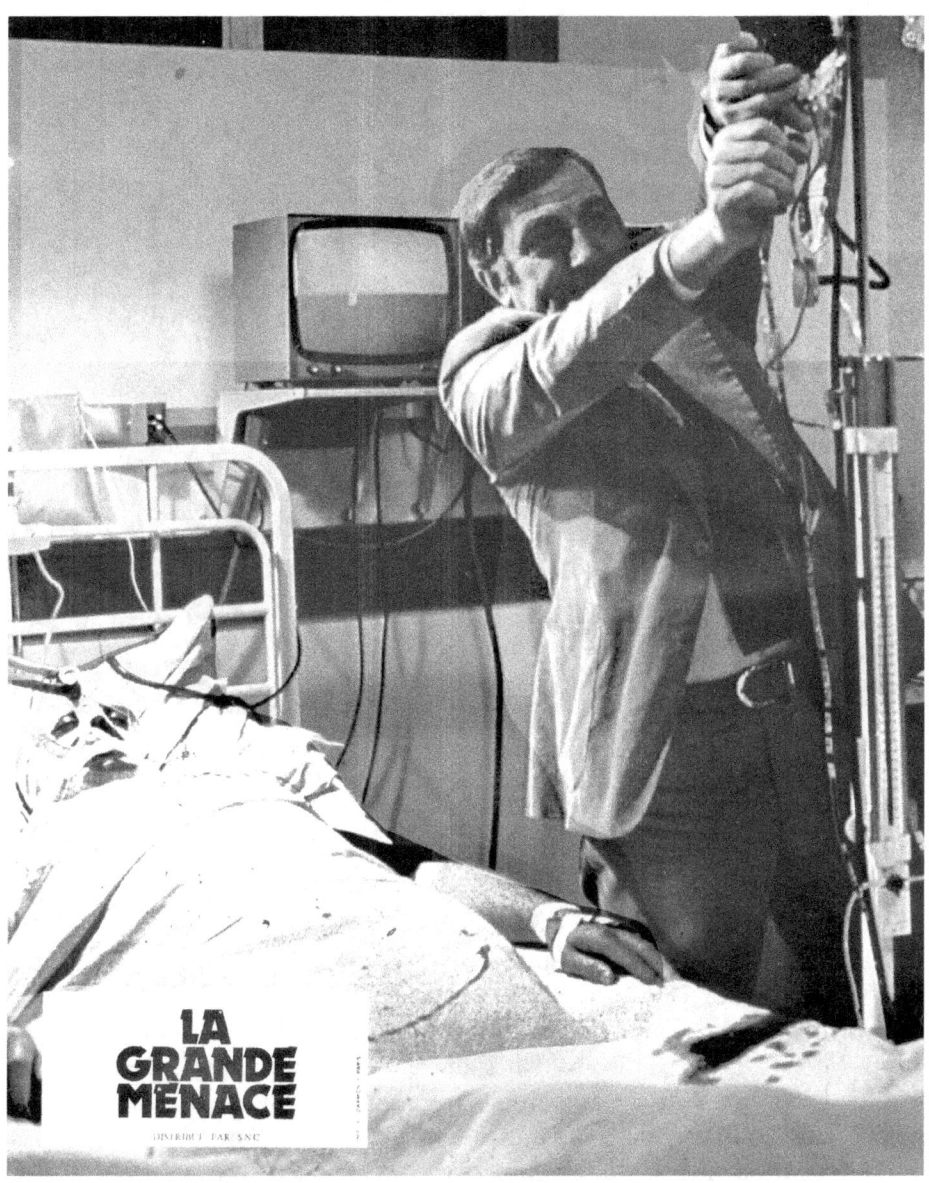

Brunel frantically tries to destroy Morlar's brain waves.

plight and, immediately afterward, disheartened to hear that he is still alive. She also must imply in her demeanor not only that she is concealing information from Brunel but that this is a terrible burden for her to endure. Her fate is a truly sad one because the incident that Morlar forced her to witness change her from a healer to a destroyer. Consequently, she sees no solution for her actions or her guilt, other than a drastic one. Remick's performance is a multi-faceted one and the fact that her role often requires her to serve as an

Morlar defends Loveless (James Hazeldine) with an impassioned antiestablishment speech; Loveless is in the row behind Morlar, next to the police officer.

apparently objective relator of past events, while concealing her own involvement, makes her achievement even more impressive.

Eminent British actors in supporting roles contribute enormously to the film's impact with Harry Andrews as the Assistant Commissioner, Gordon Jackson as Dr. Johnson and Michael Byrne as Duff having the more substantial parts. Michael Hordern, Marie-Christine Barrault, Alan Badel, Derek Jacobi, Jeremy Brett and Robert Lang are among the many fine performers who appear in the flashback sequences and enhance the film's plausibility.

John Morlar is a tragic character who was cursed with a power that he never wanted. During the course of his life, he progresses from a sensitive child to a defender of justice, from a callous cynic to a vengeful executioner. He eventually embraces the paranormal powers that he formerly cursed and utilizes them to punish the human race for which he has so much contempt, the same human race that he formerly tried to protect from the corrupt establishment. In effect, he becomes exactly what he so passionately criticized and fought against all of his adult life. He appoints himself God and, like the establishment that he despises, he becomes a mass murderer of innocent people.

The Medusa Touch is an outstanding film that builds slowly and effectively to a spectacular and horrifying climax. The movie includes many brilliant scenes of suspense and horror but the moment when Morlar's eyes suddenly open beneath the bandages is perhaps the most memorable.

Credits: Presenters: Sir Lew Grade, Elliott Kastner; Executive Producer: Arnon Milchan; Producers: Anne V. Coates, Jack Gold; Director: Jack Gold; Screenplay: John Briley, based upon a novel by Peter Van Greenaway; Supervising Editor: Anne V. Coates; Editor: Ian Crafford; Cinematography: Arthur Ibbetson; Music: Michael J. Lewis; Special Effects: Brian Johnson, Nick Allder; Visual Effects: Doug Ferris; Model Makers: Martin Bower, Bill Pearson; Art Direction: Peter Mullins

Cast: Richard Burton (John Morlar); Lino Ventura (Inspector Brunel); Lee Remick (Dr. Zonfeld); Harry Andrews (Assistant Commissioner); Gordon Jackson (Dr. Johnson); Michael Byrne (Sergeant Duff); Marie-Christine Barrault (Patricia Morlar); Jeremy Brett (Parrish); Robert Lang (Pennington); Avril Elgar (Mrs. Pennington); Alan Badel (Barrister); Derek Jacobi (Publisher); Michael Hordern (Fortune Teller); Robert Flemying (Judge McKinley); James Hazeldine (Loveless); John Normington (Schoolmaster); Norman Bird (Mr. Morlar); Jennifer Jayne (Mrs. Morlar); Frances Tomelty (Nanny); Cornelius Bowe (John Age 5); Adam Bridges (John aged 10); Joseph Clarke (John aged 14)

Afterword

The movies discussed in the preceding pages reflect an era in which science fiction movies depended upon *ideas* and not special effects; it was an era in which horror movies depended upon the power of *suggestion* and not graphic gore. Those days are gone forever. In today's Hollywood, nothing is implied anymore; everything is explicit. All of the movies in this book involve adult themes that mature audiences comprehend because the filmmakers respected their intelligence and their ability to read between the lines when necessary, metaphorically speaking.

At least some of us who wax nostalgic can relive those days from the past by watching these movies again. But how long will we be able to do this? There are some signs that Orwell's erasure of history has begun. And it is not just historical facts that are being expunged. All types of popular culture from the past, including motion pictures, are being subjected to microscopic examination to detect any sign of political, sexual or social incorrectness. Certain movies are already being banned or preceded by cautionary warnings of possible offensive content.

In view of this, it may be necessary to view the movies discussed in this volume as soon as possible because there is a good chance that they might not be available in the future. It is quite possible that some people may demand the removal of *Journey to the Far Side of the Sun* because the astronauts don't reflect diversity. Feminists will probably protest *The Mind Benders* due to its portrayal of a subservient, long-suffering wife. Satanists will almost certainly be offended by the negative portrayal of the devil in *Alias Nick Beal*. *The Maze* could be banned because it offends a potential militant group called People for the Ethical Treatment of Frogs. And *1984* will certainly be censored because...well, it's *1984*. However, there is probably no chance that *Crack in the World* will be banned because environmentalists will joyfully applaud the destruction of the earth by Mother Nature. By the way, will masculinists object to the term 'Mother Nature?'

So enjoy the movies while you can. They will excite, thrill, frighten and alarm you. But most of all, they will entertain you. At least I hope they will.

The book-burning firemen in *Fahrenheit 451*

BANNED BOOKS
and challenged

BANNED CLASSICS

1984 by George Orwell
All the King's Men by Robert Penn Warren
Animal Farm by George Orwell
As I Lay Dying by William Faulkner
Brave New World by Aldous Huxley
Call of the Wild, The by Jack London
Catch-22 by Joseph Heller
Catcher in the Rye, The by J.D. Salinger
Cat's Cradle by Kurt Vonnegut
Clockwork Orange by Anthony Burgess
Farewell to Arms, A by Ernest Hemingway
For Whom the Bell Tolls by Ernest Hemingway
Gone with the Wind by Margaret Mitchell
Grapes of Wrath, The by John Steinbeck
Great Gatsby, The by F. Scott Fitzgerald
In Cold Blood by Truman Capote
Invisible Man by Ralph Ellison
Jungle, The by Upton Sinclair
Lord of the Flies, The by William Golding
Lord of the Rings, The by J.R.R. Tolkien
Naked and the Dead, The by Norman Mailer
Naked Lunch by William S. Burroughs
Of Mice and Men by John Steinbeck
One Flew Over the Cuckoo's Nest by Ken Kesey
Separate Peace, A by John Knowles
Slaughterhouse-Five by Kurt Vonnegut
Sun Also Rises, The by Ernest Hemingway
Their Eyes Were Watching God by Zora Neale Hurston
To Kill a Mockingbird by Harper Lee

BANNED CONTEMPORARIES

Absolutely True Diary of a Part-Time Indian, The by Sherman Alexie
Alice (series) by Phyllis Reynolds Naylor
Always Running by Luis Rodriguez
Angus, Thongs, and Full-Frontal Snogging by Louise Rennison
Are You There, God? It's Me, Margaret. by Judy Blume
Arming America by Michael Bellasiles
Athletic Shorts by Chris Crutcher
Bless Me, Ultima by Rudolfo Anaya
Blood and Chocolate by Annette Curtis Klause
Blubber by Judy Blume
Boy Meets Boy by David Levithan
Boy Who Lost His Face, The Louis Sachar
Bridge to Terabithia by Katherine Paterson
Chocolate War, The by Robert Cormier
Color of Earth (series), The by Kim Dong Hwa

THE WORST THING ABOUT CENSORSHIP IS ▮▮▮▮.

Crank by Ellen Hopkins
Crazy Lady! by Jane Leslie Conly
Cut by Patricia McCormick
Day No Pigs Would Die, A by Robert Newton Peck
Detour for Emmy by Marilyn Reynolds
Earth, My Butt, and Other Big, Round Things, The by Carolyn Mackler
Face on the Milk Carton, The by Caroline B. Cooney
Fallen Angels by Walter Dean Meyers
Fat Kid Rules the World by K.L. Going
Fighting Ground, The by Avi
Flashcards of My Life by Charise Mericle Harper
Forever by Judy Blume
Friday Night Lights by H.G. Bissenger
Glass Castle, The by Jeanette Walls
Go Ask Alice by Anonymous
Golden Compass, The by Philip Pullman
Gossip Girls (series) by Cecily Von Ziegesar
Harry Potter (series) by J.K. Rowling
His Dark Materials (trilogy) by Philip Pullman
Hunger Games, The (trilogy) by Suzanne Collins
I Know Why the Caged Bird Sings by Maya Angelou
In the Night Kitchen by Maurice Sendak
It's Perfectly Normal by Robie Harris
Julie of the Wolves by Jean Craighead George
Kaffir Boy by Mark Mathabane
Killing Mr. Griffen by Lois Duncan
King & King by Linda de Haan
Life Is Funny by E.R. Frank
Looking for Alaska by John Green
Lush by Natasha Friend
My Brother Sam Is Dead by James Lincoln Collier
My Sister's Keeper by Jodi Picoult
Nickel and Dimed by Barbara Ehrenreich
Olive's Ocean by Kevin Henkes
Pact, The by Jodi Picoult
Perks of Being a Wallflower, The by Stephen Chbosky
Rainbow Boys by Alex Sanchez
Revolutionary Voices (edited) by Amy Sonnie
Roll of Thunder, Hear My Cry by Mildred D. Taylor
Scary Stories (series) by Alvin Schwartz
Snow Falling on Cedars by David Gutterson
Speak by Laurie Halse Anderson
Staying Fat for Sarah Byrnes by Chris Crutcher
Summer of My German Soldier by Bette Greene
Taming the Star Runner by S.E. Hinton
Terrorist, The by Caroline B. Cooney
Things They Carried, The by Tim O'Brien
Thirteen Reasons Why by Jay Asher
Time to Kill, A by John Grisham
ttyl; ttfn; l8r, g8r (series) by Lauren Myracle
Twilight (series) by Stephenie Meyer
Uncle Bobby's Wedding by Sarah S. Brannen
We All Fall Down by Robert Cormier
Whale Talk by Chris Crutcher
What My Mother Doesn't Kno Sonya Sones
Will Grayson, Will Grayson b, Green

Appendix

Because the genres of science fiction and horror often overlap, the inclusion of many films within specific categories is subjective. To avoid revealing how much of my life I have spent in movie theaters enjoying journeys into supernatural and extraterrestrial realms, I have restricted full disclosure of my celluloid adventures by omitting the following categories: monster movies, including such classics as *King Kong* (1933) and *Creature from the Black Lagoon* (1954), because they are too monstrous; fantasy movies, including such classics as *The Thief of Bagdad* (1940) and *Jason and the Argonauts* (1963), because they are too fantastic; and Hitchcock movies, including such classics as *Psycho* (1960) and *The Birds* (1963), because they are too Hitchcockian.

My Favorite Science Fiction Movies
1 - Invasion of the Body Snatchers (1956)
2 - This Island Earth (1955)
3 - The Day the Earth Stood Still (1951)
4 - The War of the Worlds (1953)
5 - Forbidden Planet (1956)
6 - The Thing from Another World (1951)
7 - Planet of the Apes (1968)
8 - The Incredible Shrinking Man (1957)
9 - Rocketship X-M (1950)
10 - It Came from Outer Space (1953)

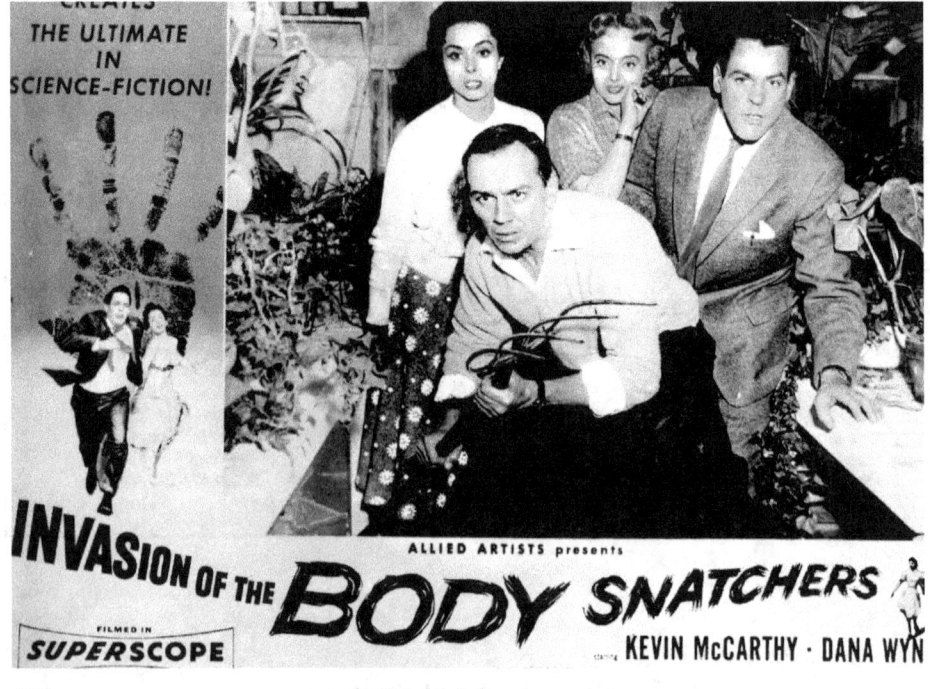

Runners-Up: (listed chronologically)
The Invisible Man (1933)
Invaders from Mars (1953)
Donovan's Brain (1953)
The Creeping Unknown aka The Quatermass Xperiment (1955)
1984 (1956)
Enemy from Space aka Quatermass 2 (1957)
The Fly (1958)
Village of the Damned (1960)
These Are the Damned aka The Damned (1962)
First Men in the Moon (1964)
Seconds (1966)
Five Million Years to Earth aka Quatermass and the Pit (1967)
The Power (1968)
The Groundstar Conspiracy (1972)
Conquest of the Planet of the Apes (1972)
Soylent Green (1973)
Who? (1974)
Capricorn One (1977)
Lifeforce (1985)

My Favorite Horror Movies
1 - Horror of Dracula aka Dracula (1958)
2 - Curse of the Werewolf (1961)
3 - Frankenstein (1931)
4 - The Curse of Frankenstein (1957)
5 - Dracula (1979)
6 - The Wolf Man (1941)
7 - The Bride of Frankenstein (1935)
8 - Son of Dracula (1943)
9 - The Medusa Touch (1978)
10 - Son of Frankenstein (1939)

Runners-Up: (listed chronologically)
Dracula (1931)
Dr. Jekyll and Mr. Hyde (1931)
The Mummy (1932)
Island of Lost Souls (1932)
The Black Cat (1934)
Cat People (1942)
Alias Nick Beal (1949)
House of Wax (1953)
The Maze (1953)

The Revenge of Frankenstein (1958)
The Mummy (1959)
The Brides of Dracula (1960)
Kiss of the Vampire (1963)
The Masque of the Red Death (1964)
The Gorgon (1964)
The Skull (1965)
The Devil's Bride aka The Devil Rides Out (1968)
Frankenstein Must Be Destroyed (1969)
Tales from the Crypt (1972)
Theater of Blood (1973)

Some Great Performances by an Actor in a Science Fiction Movie
1 - Kevin McCarthy (Invasion of the Body Snatchers; 1956)
2 - Jeff Morrow (This Island Earth; 1955)
3 - Michael Rennie (The Day the Earth Stood Still; 1951)
4 - Grant Williams (The Incredible Shrinking Man; 1957)
5 - Charlton Heston (Planet of the Apes; 1968)
6 - Walter Pidgeon (Forbidden Planet; 1956)
7 - James Donald (Five Million Years to Earth; 1967)
8 - Edmond O'Brien (1984; 1956)

9 - George Sanders (Village of the Damned; 1960)
10 - Gene Barry (The War of the Worlds; 1953)

Runners-Up: (listed chronologically)
Claude Rains (The Invisible Man; 1933)
Morris Ankrum (Rocketship X-M; 1950)
Richard Carlson (The Maze; 1953)
Rod Taylor (The Time Machine; 1960)
Ray Milland (X: The Man With X-Ray Eyes; 1963)
Edward Judd (First Men in the Moon; 1964)
Lionel Jeffries (First Men in the Moon; 1964)
Paul Mantee (Robinson Crusoe on Mars; 1964)
Dana Andrews (Crack in the World; 1965)
Rock Hudson (Seconds; 1966)
George Hamilton (The Power; 1968)
Patrick Wymark (Journey to the Far Side of the Sun aka Doppelgänger; 1969)
Bruce Dern (Silent Running; 1972)
Michael Sarrazin (The Groundstar Conspiracy; 1972)
The Day of the Dolphin (1973)
Joseph Bova (Who?; 1974)

Some Great Performances by an Actor in a Horror Movie

Note: Peter Cushing created two iconic portrayals (Dr. Van Helsing and Dr. Frankenstein) and it was difficult choosing which to include on this list so I have allowed the flip of a coin to select the former.

1 - Peter Cushing (Horror of Dracula; 1958)
2 - Oliver Reed (Curse of the Werewolf; 1961)
3 - Boris Karloff (Frankenstein; 1932)
4 - George C. Scott (The Changeling; 1980)
5 - Christopher Lee (Horror of Dracula; 1958)
6 - Richard Burton (The Medusa Touch; 1978)
7 - Basil Rathbone (Son of Frankenstein; 1939)
8 - Frank Langella (Dracula; 1979)
9 - Robert Paige (Son of Dracula; 1943)
10 - Vincent Price (The Masque of the Red Death; 1964)

Runners-Up: (listed chronologically)
Fredric March (Dr. Jekyll and Mr. Hyde; 1931)
Charles Laughton (Island of Lost Souls; 1932)
Bela Lugosi (Son of Frankenstein; 1939)
Lon Chaney, Jr. (Son of Dracula; 1943)
Henry Daniell (The Body Snatcher; 1945)

Lew Ayres (Donovan's Brain; 1953)
David Peel (The Brides of Dracula; 1960)
Clifford Evans (Curse of the Werewolf; 1961)
Noel Willman (Kiss of the Vampire; 1963)
Andrew Keir (Dracula, Prince of Darkness; 1966)
Eric Braeden (Colossus: The Forbin Project; 1970)
John Ryan (It's Alive; 1974)

Some Great Performances by an Actress in a Science Fiction Movie
1 - Barbara Shelley (Five Million Years to Earth; 1967)
2 - Patricia Neal (The Day the Earth Stood Still; 1951)
3 - Jan Sterling (1984; 1956)
4 - Osa Massen (Rocketship X-M; 1950)
5 - Viveca Lindfors (These Are the Damned; 1961)
6 - Patricia Owens (The Fly; 1958)
7 - Ann Robinson (The War of the Worlds; 1953)
8 - Christine Belford (The Groundstar Conspiracy; 1972)
9 - Dana Wynter (Invasion of the Body Snatchers; 1956)
10 - Gloria Talbott (I Married a Monster from Outer Space; 1958)

Some Great Performances by an Actress in a Horror Movie
1 - Elsa Lanchester (The Bride of Frankenstein; 1935)
2 - Simone Simon (Cat People; 1942)
3 - Louise Albritton (Son of Dracula; 1943)
4 - Julie Harris (The Haunting; 1963)
5 - Deborah Kerr (The Innocents; 1961)
6 - Diana Rigg (Theater of Blood; 1973)
7 - Martita Hunt (The Brides of Dracula; 1960)
8 - Kim Hunter (The Seventh Victim; 1943)
9 - Sharon Farrell (It's Alive; 1974)
10 - Ingrid Pitt (Countess Dracula; 1971)

**Visit
www.midmar.com
for a complete listing
of our books
or visit Midnight Marquee
on Amazon.com**

www.ingramcontent.com/pod-product-compliance
Lightning Source LLC
Chambersburg PA
CBHW072001070526
44583CB00015B/1281